Frank Lehmann

Behind the Scripts – Stories in Progress

Vol. 1

AF208818

Frank Lehmann

BEHIND THE SCRIPTS – STORIES IN PROGRESS
VOL. 1

Welcome to a book that offers more than just screenplays – it provides an exclusive glimpse into the very first drafts of two film projects. If you're passionate about the creative process behind a film and want to experience how an idea evolves into a living story, then this book is for you.

This book is for readers who don't just consume stories but engage with them, feel them, and want to be part of their development. It's for those who appreciate the raw, unpolished energy of a first screenplay draft and enjoy witnessing the journey from concept to completion. Here, you won't find polished, meticulously refined scripts – but rather exciting blueprints that still have room to grow.

We invite you to be part of the journey. Your thoughts, feedback, and enthusiasm can help shape these projects into films. Let's create stories together that captivate and inspire.

Enjoy the read and the discovery!

Bibliografische Information der Deutschen Nationalbibliothek: Die Deutsche Nationalbibliothek verzeichnet diese Publikation in der Deutschen Nationalbibliografie; detaillierte bibliografische Daten sind im Internet über http://dnb.dnb.de abrufbar.

Verlag: BoD · Books on Demand GmbH, In de Tarpen 42, 22848 Norderstedt, bod@bod.de

Druck: Libri Plureos GmbH, Friedensallee 273, 22763 Hamburg

ISBN: 978-3-7597-3120-3

Table of Contents

Pitch Deck

Tagline:
"There are evils that never die—they just wait."

Logline

When **Alice Walker**'s son, Dennis, disappears at a derelict psychiatric clinic, she teams up with police officer **Steve Miles** to uncover a dreadful, ancient force that claims its victims in a place of shadows. Their only hope of ending this evil may require burning down the very site of its power—yet it won't bring Dennis back.

Brief Synopsis

- **Setup**: Alice, a single mother, searches for her 20-year-old son Dennis, who vanished while exploring a "Lost Place" with his friend Tom. The local police are indifferent, until Steve Miles listens to her pleas.

- **Conflict**: Clues lead to an abandoned psychiatric clinic with a disturbing record of vanishings. Professor Livingston reveals a centuries-old Inca-related curse (Supay) bound to the clinic, devouring anyone who dares enter.

- **Tension Escalation**: Several teens, including the mayor's daughter Amelia, throw a covert party in the clinic. They are attacked by horrifying shadow creatures lurking within.

- **Climax**: Realizing bullets do nothing and that the monsters fear fire, Alice and Steve soak the building in gasoline, setting it ablaze to destroy the demon.

- **Outcome**: The clinic is consumed by flames, presumably eradicating the supernatural threat. Official reports blame a catastrophic fire and "mass hallucinations." Alice returns to her old life, unable to save Dennis, but ensuring no one else will fall prey to that horror.

Genre & Tone

- **Genre**: Horror / Supernatural Thriller

- **Tone**:

  - Intensely atmospheric, mixing psychological dread with monstrous encounters.

  - Grounded emotional core through Alice's maternal anguish.

  - Mythic flair via an Inca curse, blending real-world believability with dark mysticism.

Target Audience

- **Age Range**: Horror fans, 16+ or 18+ depending on intensity.

- **Interests**: Supernatural/haunted settings, folklore-based horror (akin to *Silent Hill*, *Evil Dead*, *Insidious*), plus a relatable emotional hook.

- **Market**: Ideal for genre festivals, theatrical or streaming (Netflix, Shudder, Amazon Prime), strong potential for global appeal.

Unique Selling Points (USP)

1. **Emotional Core**: A mother's desperate search for her missing son imbues the horror with deep stakes.

2. **Lost Place Setting**: An abandoned clinic, an illicit teenage party, and a hidden demon—a potent blend of youth culture and supernatural terror.

3. **Inca Mythology**: Supay (god of the underworld) adds a distinctive cultural edge, elevating the film above standard ghost stories.

4. **Fire Finale**: Dramatic, visually striking climax—fire versus darkness—that seals the demon's fate in a literal blaze.

Visual Concept

- **Look & Feel**:

    o   Decaying corridors, dusty wards, flickering neon or emergency lights.

    o   Color palette: cold greens/blues by night, contrasting with the orange glow of muzzle flashes and the final blazing fire.

    o   Monsters as semi-seen shadows with black "vein-like" growths.

- **Atmosphere**:

    o   Hybrid of classic haunted-house horror and gritty police procedural.

Key Characters

- **Alice Walker**: Determined single mother, evolving from uncertain to fearless in her quest to save Dennis and others.

- **Steve Miles**: Empathetic cop, drawn into an unimaginable threat, becomes Alice's staunch ally.

- **Professor Theodor Livingston**: Once led the clinic, inadvertently locked in a curse from a doomed patient, O'Kelly.

- **Amelia**: The mayor's daughter, celebrating her 18th birthday in the clinic—only to face unimaginable terror.

- **Mayor Donald Abraham**: Tries to dismiss "rumors" to protect the town, but panics when Amelia is endangered.

Budget & Production

- **Budget Range**: Low-to-mid for a horror film, depending on VFX/practical effects.

    o   Key emphasis on an **evocative location** (the abandoned clinic) and **practical monster FX**.

- **Locations**:

    o   Abandoned building or studio sets for the clinic's interior.

- ○ Police station, mayor's home, external city streets.

- ○ Minimal reliance on big sets beyond the core haunted environment.

Conclusion / Appeal

"**Shadows of the Clinic**" merges classic haunted-house dread with a mother's heart-wrenching drama, spiced by an underutilized Inca mythological threat. Combining emotional stakes—Alice's desperate search for her son—and harrowing set pieces—teenagers facing a horrific demise—offers a gripping horror experience. The flaming finale is equal parts visual spectacle and narrative catharsis. This film aims to satisfy horror purists while capturing mainstream viewers with its deeply human storyline.

Ready to torch the darkness and conquer this evil once and for all?

SCRIPT

HAUNTING DEPTHS - SUPAY´S REALM

Written by Frank Lehmann

First Draft 01.11.2025

Freiwasser Filmproduktion
Metelsdorfer Str. 2b
23972 Dorf Mecklenburg
GERMANY

Phone: +49 178 1339406
Mail: info@frank-lehmann.biz

EXT. ABANDONED PSYCHIATRIC CLINIC – LATE AFTERNOON

A decrepit psychiatric clinic looms at the end of an overgrown path. TOM (20) and DENNIS (20) stand before its massive, weathered door. Each holds a camera. They share an excited, mischievous grin.

                    TOM (INTO HIS CAMERA)
          This is insane! Look at this place, Dennis!

                    DENNIS (RAISING HIS CAMERA)
          Lost Place number seven—this is

          gonna be our highlight reel!

They set their shoulders and push the heavy door. It creaks open, stirring dust motes in the fading light.

INT. ABANDONED PSYCHIATRIC CLINIC – HALLWAY – LATE AFTERNOON

Their flashlights sweep across peeling wallpaper, broken furniture, and scattered debris. Their voices echo, full of nervous laughter.

                    DENNIS
          I'm sending a video to my mom. She's gonna
          freak when she sees where we are.

Dennis checks his phone. No signal.

                    DENNIS (QUIET FRUSTRATION) (CONT'D)
          Damn. No reception. I'll step outside for a
          sec.

Tom nods, distracted by an old medical cabinet. Dennis slips out.

EXT. ABANDONED PSYCHIATRIC CLINIC – EARLY EVENING

Dennis stands in the dimming light, illuminated by the glow of his phone's screen. He quickly sends the video. Relieved, he heads back in.

INT. ABANDONED PSYCHIATRIC CLINIC – HALLWAY – EARLY EVENING

Dennis returns, expecting Tom's eager chatter. Instead—silence.

                    DENNIS

        Tom? Hey, where'd you go?

He searches room after room. On the floor: TOM'S BACKPACK and a FLASHLIGHT still shining.

                    DENNIS (UNDER HIS BREATH) (CONT'D)

        What the hell...?

A faint, scratching whisper radiates from the shadows. Dennis lifts the flashlight, pointing it toward the sound.

Black, pulsating veins spread across the walls, creeping closer with unsettling speed.

                    DENNIS (SHAKEN) (CONT'D)

        Oh God…

He staggers back. The flashlight slips from his hand and lands on the floor. In its narrow beam, a zombie-like figure scuttles past.

Dennis screams—raw and terrified—and then, abruptly, silence.

Only the flashlight remains, illuminating empty space and the distant echo of something dreadful that just happened.

EXT. COUNTRY ROAD / FOREST – DAY (DRONE SHOT)

A compact car glides along a winding country road, flanked by dense forest. From high above, the lush canopy spreads out below. TITLE and CREDITS appear on screen as the car continues on its path.

The view follows the car into a small TOWN, still from the air. It cruises down the main street, passing modest shops and cottages, finally coming to a stop in front of the PO-LICE STATION.

The car halts. <u>END DRONE SHOT.</u>

EXT. POLICE STATION - DAY

At ground level, ALICE (38) steps out of the car. She closes the door firmly and walks toward the station´s entrance, determination in every step.

INT. POLICE STATION – DAY

A busy open-plan office. SEVERAL OFFICERS at their desks, typing reports, sorting through files. Computers hum softly, a ceiling fan turns lazily. At the entrance, behind a COUNTER, a DESK OFFICER (50) reads a newspaper.

ALICE (38) enters. Concern and determination etched on her face, she heads straight for the counter.

> ALICE
>
> Excuse me, I'm looking for my son, Dennis Walker. He and his friend Tom have been missing for two months. I've got a lead that they were last seen in this area.

The DESK OFFICER lowers his newspaper, sighing as if irritated.

> DESK OFFICER
>
> Sorry, ma'am. Can't help you with that.
>
> (calls over his shoulder) Petersen! Could you handle this?

At the back of the room, a door opens: STEVE MILES (42) steps out of the HANK OBAMA'S OFFICE. Holding a few files, he moves toward his desk, right next to OFFICER PETERSEN (35). He settles in quietly, observing the exchange from a short distance.

ALICE looks uncertain, then walks over to PETERSEN's desk. PETERSEN barely acknowledges her presence.

> PETERSEN
> What's this about?

ALICE

My son Dennis and his friend Tom disappeared two
months ago. Dennis sent me this video of them ente-
ring an old clinic nearby. He's registered as missing
in London. Please, I need your help.

She shows PETERSEN a photo of DENNIS and TOM and the VIDEO on her phone.
PETERSEN gives it a cursory glance.

STEVE, now seated at his desk, pretends to flip through documents but is actually listening closely. He frowns at his colleague's dismissive attitude.

PETESEN
(sighing)

We've had all the info from London PD. No sign of
your boys here.

PETERSEN (CONT'D)

They probably just took off. Happens all the time.
People vanish and then turn up later.

ALICE's voice trembles with anxiety.

ALICE

You don't understand—this clinic, something's
wrong! I need you to look into it.

PETERSEN raises a hand dismissively.

PETERSEN

Ma'am, without concrete evidence, there's not
much we can do. Our resources are limited. Trust
the authorities.

ALICE is on the verge of tears, yet tries to remain composed.

ALICE But
my son—

PETERSEN glances at the clock, impatient.

PETERSEN

I'm on break now. Sorry.

ALICE stands there, devastated. She turns and walks toward the exit. STEVE watches her go, sensing her despair. He says nothing but his tight jaw and narrowed eyes reveal his disapproval. As ALICE reaches the door, STEVE shakes his head slightly, then returns to his files, already considering how he might take action on his own.

EXT. POLICE STATION – DAY

The police station door swings open. ALICE (38) steps out, the sunlight catching her eyes. She walks to her car parked nearby, shoulders squared, her face a mask of controlled resolve. Still, there's a tension in her eyes that betrays her inner turmoil.

She gets in, closes the door. For a moment, she breaks down completely, tears streaming down her cheeks. Her breath comes in shaky gasps. After a few moments, she wipes her face, checking her reflection in the rearview mirror, determined to regain composure.

ALICE picks up her PHONE and dials. It rings

ALICE (TRYING TO SOUND CALM)

Hello? Yes, it's Alice… I just wanted to let you
know I'm here. I spoke with the police, but…
they're not taking this seriously. I'm so sorry.
Look, I'm not giving up. I'm going to stay here,
find a room, and keep looking for Dennis and
Tom. I won't stop, okay?

She listens, nodding as though the other person could see her.

ALICE

Yes, I'll call you again as soon as I have any news.
Thank you… Take care. Bye.

She ends the call, starts the engine, and pulls onto the main street. The car glides through the small town until the buildings give way to the sights of the HARBOR ahead. Alice´s gaze remains steady, determined.

INT. SMALL HOTEL AT THE HARBOR – DAY

A cozy lobby with warm lighting. Through a large window near the reception desk, sunlight filters in, revealing a view of the harbor. Next to the desk is a small table where two GUESTS (in their 30s) browse brochures and quietly discuss the local attractions.

ALICE (38) enters, carrying a travel bag. She appears determined but maintains a polite demeanor. Behind the RECEPTION stands SARAH (27), smiling warmly.

                    SARAH

          Good afternoon, welcome! How can I help you?

                    ALICE

          Good afternoon. I'd like a room, please—just for
          three nights to start.

Sarah inputs some details into the computer, her smile never fading.

                    SARAH

          No problem. We have a lovely room overlooking the
          harbor. May I have your name?

                    ALICE

          Alice Walker.

Sarah types a bit more, then retri ves a key.

                    SARAH

          Ms. Walker, here are your keys. You'll find your room
          on the first floor. Just take the stairs next to the re-
          ception desk. Your room number is 12.

Alice takes the key, then hesitates slightly before asking:

                    ALICE

          One more thing—do you know anything about mis-
                              sing persons in this area?

17

Sarah shakes her head, still polite and composed.

                    SARAH

        I'm sorry, not that I know of. Is everything all right?

Alice offers a faint smile.

                    ALICE

        Yes, thank you. I was just curious. Thanks again.

She picks up her bag and heads upstairs. The guests at the table continue murmuring softly among themselves as Sarah returns to her tasks.

INT. HOTEL ROOM – DAY

ALICE (38) enters the room, setting her travel bag on a chair beside a small table. The space is sparsely furnished but clean and cozy. There's a double bed, a small wardrobe, a bedside table with a lamp. Warm hues on the walls give a soft, welcoming glow despite the simplicity.

She surveys the room, takes a quick look into the adjacent bathroom, then moves past the double bed to the window. Pulling the curtain aside, she gazes out: boats in the harbor, a gentle breeze rippling the water's surface. Under different circumstances, it would be a peaceful, picturesque scene.

Allowing the curtain to fall back, ALICE sits on the bed. She takes out her phone and plays the last video she received from DENNIS and TOM. Tears well in her eyes as their familiar voices and faces flicker across the screen.

Overcome by sorrow and fatigue, she places the phone on the bedside table. Rolling onto her side, she lets the tears stream silently down her face. Eventually, she cries herself into a fitful sleep.

INT. HARBOR BAR – EVENING

The bar is lively. LOCALS and TOURISTS chat, laugh, and enjoy the energetic atmosphere. On a small stage, a MUSICIAN (30) plays guitar and sings modern rock-pop tunes, filling the room with a vibrant mood.

ALICE (38) enters and takes a brief look around before heading to the bar. The BARTENDER (40) greets her with a friendly smile.

BARTENDER

Good evening. What can I get you?

ALICE (SLIGHTLY WEARY)

A cocktail, please. Something with rum and pinea-
pple.

As the BARTENDER mixes the drink, he studies ALICE briefly.

BARTENDER

New in town?

ALICE (NODDING)

Yes, I just arrived today.

BARTENDER (FRIENDLY)

Welcome to Pearl Harbor. It's usually quiet here,
but the nights can be quite lively.

ALICE takes the cocktail, thanks him, and moves to a table by the window. She sips her
drink, observing the crowd, though worry lingers in her eyes.

INT. HARBOR BAR – LATER

The door opens again. STEVE MILES (42) enters, acknowledging some colleagues
with a curt nod. He notices ALICE at the window, hesitates briefly, then approaches
and stands beside her table.

STEVE (CAUTIOUSLY SMILING)

Is this seat taken?

ALICE (DISMISSIVE)

I'm sorry, but I'd rather be alone.

STEVE remains, meeting her gaze seriously.

STEVE (EARNEST)

I'm sorry to intrude. I'm Steve Miles, a police
officer here in Pearl Harbor. I overheard your
conversation at the station this morning. You're
Alice Walker, right?

ALICE looks up, surprised and wary. After a moment, she nods.

ALICE (RESERVED)

That's me. What do you want?

STEVE (GENTLE)

I just wanted to say I'm sorry about how my colleagues treated your case. I'd like to help you, if you'll
let me.

ALICE studies him, takes a deep breath. Her posture relaxes slightly.

ALICE (RELIEVED)

Please, have a seat. I could use all the help I
can get.

STEVE sits down, signals a passing WAITER for a beer. They sit quietly for a moment, listening to the music, watching the patrons. Then STEVE speaks again, more
softly.

STEVE (EMPATHETIC)

I understand you're looking for your son. I'm sorry
my colleagues weren't more supportive. I want to
help you.

ALICE (GRATEFUL)

That means a lot. It's so frustrating not
being taken

seriously. Dennis is everything to me. I have to
know what happened.

ALICE shows STEVE her phone, displaying a photo of DENNIS and TOM standing in
front of a rundown clinic. STEVE studies it thoughtfully.

STEVE (THOUGHTFUL)

That's the old psychiatric clinic on the outskirts of
town. People avoid it—some say it's haunted. But I
suspect there's more to it.

ALICE (CONCERNED)

Dennis and Tom wanted to explore abandoned
places. Do you think we'll find clues there?

STEVE (DETERMINED)

That clinic has a dark history.

There are rumors of strange lights, noises, and missing people. I think it's worth checking out tomorrow.

ALICE (HOPEFUL)

Really? That would be wonderful. I don't know who
else to turn to.

STEVE (REASSURING)

I'll be outside your hotel in the morning. We won't
leave any stone unturned.

ALICE's eyes shine with relief and gratitude as STEVE offers a slight smile. The MUSI-
CIAN continues to play gentle rock-pop melodies, and a quiet sense of understanding
settles between them—a spark of hope in the midst of uncertainty.

INT. STEVE'S APARTMENT – BEDROOM – NIGHT

Dim LIGHT. STEVE (42) and AMANDA (42) lie in a disheveled BED, suggesting recent
intimacy. STEVE sits partially upright, a PILLOW propped behind him, staring thoughtfully at the CEILING. AMANDA leans against his shoulder, restless. Her fingers fiddle
nervously with a CORNER OF THE SHEET.

For a moment, only their breathing can be heard. Then AMANDA speaks, her voice
quiet but serious.

AMANDA (SOFTLY)

Steve… I can't pretend everything's fine. I can feel there's something that's drawing you away—something bigger than us.

STEVE shifts his gaze from the ceiling, turning slightly toward her.

STEVE (HESITANT)

It's not about you, Amanda. It's just… I've got a case. A missing person case I'm diving into more than usual.

AMANDA pulls the sheets up, frustrated.

AMANDA (SLIGHTLY IRRITATED)

Steve, you and I… we've been keeping it casual. I always told myself it was enough. But if I'm honest, I was hoping you'd at least think about us in the long run.

STEVE exhales, choosing his words carefully.

STEVE (MATTER-OF-FACT)

I know. I never promised anything. This… whatever it is between us… has been uncomplicated. But now… there's someone who needs help.

Alice Walker. She's looking for her missing son and she's totally desperate.

AMANDA smirks bitterly.

AMANDA (QUIETLY)

I figured. She's the reason, isn't she? Steve, you've never been this… distracted. Not even with your other cases.

STEVE is silent for a moment, then nods slowly.

STEVE

Maybe you're right. Alice is… strong, frantic, fighting like mad for her son. I… feel I have to help her. And… (sighs) …I can't stand how people here just turn a blind eye.

AMANDA sits up, sliding away from STEVE. She looks at him intently.

                    AMANDA

          So you're already somewhere else. (pauses) You
          know what, Steve? I think we've both been lying to
          ourselves.

She stands, starts getting dressed. STEVE watches but says nothing. AMANDA gives him one last look.

               AMANDA (FLAT)(CONT'D)

          Take care of yourself. Good luck with your case.

She leaves the bedroom, the door closing softly behind her. STEVE remains behind, his head leaning against the wall, lost in thought and confronted with the stark reality of his own feelings.

EXT. IN FRONT OF THE HOTEL – MORNING

The morning sun shines brightly in a clear blue sky. Birds chirp as a gentle breeze drifts in from the lake. ALICE (38) stands outside the hotel entrance, gazing down the street, when a BLACK FORD RANGER pulls up and stops in front of her.

Behind the wheel sits STEVE MILES (42), his face illuminated by the early sunlight. He lowers the window and smiles at ALICE.

                 STEVE (FRIENDLY)

          Good morning, Alice. Ready for our little excursion?

ALICE's expression brightens, relief and hope evident for the first time in a long while.

               ALICE (SLIGHTLY SMILING)

           Good morning, Steve. Yes, I'm ready. Let's not
          waste any time.

STEVE gets out, walks around the vehicle, and opens the door for ALICE. She climbs in, and he closes the door, returning to the driver's side and starting the engine.

               STEVE (LIGHTLY JOKING)

It's a beautiful day—perfect for a bit of detective
work.

The FORD RANGER pulls away from the hotel, heading toward the old clinic. The
camera follows as it cruises through the picturesque streets of Pearl Harbor. Locals go
about their daily routines, the town appearing peaceful and welcoming.

A wide shot shows the vehicle receding into the distance, the rising sun bathing the landscape in golden light.

Inside the truck, ALICE and STEVE sit quietly side by side, their thoughts fixed on the
search ahead. Tension and hope fill the air as they move toward the unknown.

EXT. ROAD OUTSIDE PEARL HARBOR – MORNING

The FORD RANGER moves along a scenic route. Sunlight streams through the
windows, filling the interior with a warm glow. A contemplative silence hangs in the air.
ALICE (38) sits in the passenger seat, her gaze fixed outside as peaceful scenery un-
folds.

INT. FORD RANGER – MORNING

ALICE furrows her brow, staring out the window, while STEVE (42) focuses on the
road. They remain quiet for a while, until ALICE breaks the silence.

                    ALICE (HESITANT)

          Steve… what if I'm doing the wrong thing? What if
          I'm out here while Dennis is actually somewhere
          else? What if I'm too late?

STEVE glances at her briefly, empathy in his eyes.

                    STEVE (GENTLY)

          Alice, it's completely normal to have those doubts.
          But you are doing the right thing. You're not giving
          up—you're searching for your son. That takes incre-
          dible strength.

ALICE sighs, lowering her head.

                    ALICE (SOFTLY)

Sometimes I feel so helpless.

STEVE takes a deep breath, choosing his words carefully.

> STEVE (CARING)
>
> I know how that feels. I made mistakes in my youth. I was in a gang, making money from stolen cars. One night, the police caught me, while my friends got away. I never saw them again.

ALICE turns to him, startled.

> ALICE (SHOCKED)
>
> What happened to them?

STEVE keeps his eyes on the road.

> STEVE (QUIETLY)
>
> No one knows. They just vanished. I was never convicted and managed to straighten out my life. But in a small town like Pearl Harbor, people don't forget easily.

ALICE regards him with sympathy.

> ALICE (IMPRESSED)
>
> And yet you became a police
>
> officer. You didn't let your past define you.

STEVE smiles slightly.

> STEVE (SMILING)
>
> Exactly. I wanted to make a difference, to help people. Sometimes life takes us down paths we never imagined. But those paths shape us and give us the strength to keep going, even when it's hard.

ALICE nods, encouraged by his words.

> ALICE (GRATEFUL)

Thank you, Steve. Your story gives me hope. I won't
give up, no matter what happens.

STEVE casts her a determined glance.

STEVE (RESOLUTE)

And I'll help you, Alice. We'll find Dennis, no
matter what it takes.

The sun rises higher, bathing the landscape in golden light as the FORD RANGER
continues onward. The silence that now settles is no longer heavy, but filled with renewed determination and hope.

EXT. ABANDONED PSYCHIATRIC CLINIC – DAY

The FORD RANGER comes to a crunching halt in front of an imposing yet eerie building. The façade is weathered, some windows are shattered, and vines crawl up the
walls. STEVE (42) and ALICE (38) remain inside the truck, peering through the windshield at the old clinic.

A beat of silence. STEVE places a hand on the door handle, ready to get out, when
ALICE gently grabs his arm.

ALICE (QUIETLY, FEARFUL) Steve,
wait. What if we find nothing but more confusion inside? What if we just end up with more questions
instead of answers? I'm not sure I can handle that.

STEVE turns to her, understanding in his eyes.

STEVE (SOOTHING)

Alice, I understand your fear. But we're here because we're looking for Dennis. We can't just give
up. Whatever we find inside—we'll face it together.
You're not alone in this.

ALICE takes a deep breath and finally, albeit reluctantly, nods. They both step out of
the truck. A faint breeze stirs through the overgrown grounds, carrying the stale scent
of decay and neglect.

They approach the entrance. The heavy wooden door, weathered and half ajar, stands like a silent invitation. ALICE and STEVE share a nervous glance before stepping cautiously into the clinic´s dim interior.

INT. ABANDONED PSYCHIATRIC CLINIC – LOBBY – DAY

STEVE (42), followed closely by ALICE (38), cautiously steps through the half-opened door into the old clinic's lobby. A sharp sense of unease grips them immediately. The air is ice-cold, as if the chilling weight of the past still lingers here.

They move forward slowly. STEVE hands ALICE a flashlight he brought along. Their footsteps echo on the stone floor as they pick one of the corridors to explore. They only dare to shine their lights briefly into some of the rooms. Inside lie decaying beds, broken wheelchairs, rusty chairs, and dusty files scattered about—each sight intensifying their discomfort.

Dark, twisting hallways, crumbling staircases, and ancient furniture pass by as they venture deeper into the building. Upon reaching the first floor, they hear strange sounds. It's as if whispers and scratches are coming from everywhere and nowhere at once.

                    ALICE (WHISPERING)

          Steve, I… I think we should turn back. I can feel so-
          mething in these walls. Something's off here.

She gently touches the crumbling plaster. Her unease grows, and the noises do not fade. They shift unpredictably between soft murmurs and sudden, harsh scraping. ALICE is frightened, and STEVE tries to steady her.

                    STEVE (QUIET, REASSURING)

           It's okay, Alice. We don't have to
           rush this. Let's go back for now;   we
           can always return later.

They turn around, shining their lights down the path they came from. Suddenly, a dark figure darts out from a doorway!

                    ALICE (SHOUTING)

          Ah! Damn it!

STEVE jerks his flashlight upward, heart pounding. He curses under his breath, sharp and tense.

                    STEVE (ANGRY, LOUD)

What the hell?! Back off!

The MAN (PAUL, 24) flinches, throwing his hands up in shock, too startled to speak immediately. STEVE steps forward, flashlight raised like a weapon. ALICE grabs his arm, trying to pull him back.

ALICE (URGENT)
Steve, no! Stop!

PAUL stumbles back, losing his balance and falling onto his back. He raises his hands defensively, voice trembling.

PAUL (FEARFUL)

W-Wait! Please… I'm just a backpacker!

As PAUL struggles to stand, LUCY (19) hesitantly appears behind him, eyes wide, hands raised in surrender.

LUCY (TREMBLING)

We're sorry! We didn't mean to scare you!

STEVE pauses, breathing heavily. ALICE tugs him away from PAUL. For a moment, only their heavy breathing fills the space.

STEVE (THROUGH CLENCHED TEETH)
Who the hell are you?! What are you   doing here?

PAUL, still shaking, lifts his hands in a calming gesture.

PAUL (FRANTIC)

Paul… my name is Paul, this is

Lucy. We're backpackers. We look for lost places.

PAUL (FRANTIC) (CONT'D)

We heard about this clinic and… we wanted to explore it.

LUCY nods quickly, her voice strained.

LUCY (SOFTLY)

We're so sorry. We didn't think anyone else
would be here.

ALICE catches her breath, glancing at STEVE as his chest slowly heaves less violently.

ALICE (TENSE)

You nearly scared us to death! This place is dangerous. People have gone missing. We're trying to find
them.

PAUL and LUCY's expressions shift from shock to concern, their adventurous
spark gone.

PAUL (NERVOUS)

M-Missing? Here? We… we had no idea.

STEVE lowers the flashlight slowly, still tense but more in control now.

STEVE (FIRM)

You need to leave, right now. Something's
not right here.

LUCY nods, tears glistening in her eyes.

LUCY (WEAKLY)

We'll go. Thanks for warning us.

PAUL holds his hands up apologetically.

PAUL

I'm sorry. We didn't mean any trouble.

ALICE gives a curt nod and gently urges STEVE toward the staircase.

ALICE (QUIET BUT FIRM)

Come on, Steve. Let´s go.

STEVE shoots the backpackers one last, warning glare before he and ALICE move on. Behind them, PAUL and LUCY remain, frightened and now much more cautious. The eerie sounds linger in the air as ALICE and STEVE descend to the ground floor. With each step, some of the tension eases, but the uneasy feeling persists, following them out into the light of day.

EXT. ABANDONED PSYCHIATRIC CLINIC – DAY

STEVE (42) and ALICE (38) step out of the oppressive darkness of the building and into the open air. Their faces reflect the tension and unease of the experience they've just endured. Without speaking, they head briskly toward their car. The sky is overcast, the wind chilly, as if reflecting their unsettled mood.

On the first floor, PAUL (24) and LUCY (19) stand at a window, watching them leave. ALICE turns once more, glancing upward.

PAUL wraps an arm around LUCY, leans in, and whispers something to her. Then he gives ALICE a mischievous grin and a casual wave.

PAUL (QUIETLY, TO LUCY)

No way we're leaving… this place is awesome!

LUCY looks startled, but says nothing. Her loyalty to PAUL outweighs her fear.

STEVE and ALICE reach the car. STEVE opens the driver's door, and ALICE settles into the passenger seat. In silence, STEVE starts the engine and carefully turns the vehicle around. Both glance back up at the window where the backpackers just stood.

STEVE (SOFTLY, CONCERNED)

 I'm not sure they understood how dangerous this
 place is.

ALICE nods, her eyes serious.

ALICE

I hope they clear out. This place isn't right.

The car rolls away, leaving the clinic behind. PAUL and LUCY step back from the window, out of sight. The lingering unease remains as STEVE and ALICE drive off, the building and its mysteries left behind—at least for now.

EXT. FOREST ROAD – LATE AFTERNOON

The FORD RANGER travels quietly along a deserted road, surrounded by dense forest. Sunlight filters through the canopy, casting flickering shadows on the windshield. STEVE (42) focuses on the road, ALICE (38) gazes thought-fully out the window. The silence in the vehicle is broken only by the gentle hum of the engine.

                    ALICE (SOFTLY)

          Steve, I… I have this feeling that something terrible
          happened in that clinic. For the first time, I'm not sure
          I can handle it all. What if we don't find any clues
          about the boys?

STEVE gives her a brief, understanding glance before returning his eyes to the road.

                    STEVE (CALMLY)

          Alice, I understand your fears. But we're going to get
          to the bottom of this. We won't give up. We'll find out
          what happened in that clinic.

ALICE sighs, running a hand through her hair. Her eyes reflect worry and doubt.

                    ALICE (UNCERTAIN)

          But what if we find nothing? What if all my efforts
          were in vain?

STEVE briefly places a hand on her shoulder, then returns it to the wheel.

                    STEVE (REASSURING)

          Alice, because of you, I've found a purpose that
          pulls me out of my dull routine. I'm grateful for that.

ALICE looks at him, doubt still lingering, but a spark of hope emerging.

ALICE (QUIETLY)

Thank you, Steve. I appreciate your support.

STEVE meets her gaze. His expression suggests he feels more than just gratitude.

STEVE (WITH CONVICTION)

We're a team, Alice. And teams don't give up.

ALICE nods slowly. Her uncertainty gives way to a sense of connection.

ALICE (DETERMINED) I
hope you're right.

STEVE (CONFIDENT)

We'll find out. Together.

The camera pulls back as the FORD RANGER continues down the forest road. The sun sinks lower, shadows lengthen, and they move into an uncertain future—but not without hope.

INT. DINER IN PEARL HARBOR – DAY

Sunlight streams through the window, bathing the cozy diner in a warm glow. At a window table, ALICE (38) and STEVE (42) sit before steaming cups of coffee and plates of freshly baked apple pie. The soft murmur of other CUSTOMERS, the clinking of dishes, and the aroma of pastries create a calming backdrop.

ALICE (THOUGHTFUL, TAKING A BITE OF PIE)

So, how do we proceed, Steve? We need more information about that clinic.

STEVE (TURNING HIS COFFEE CUP)

Yes, definitely. I think the best approach is to track down the clinic's owner. Maybe he knows more about the building's history and what went on there.

ALICE (RAISING AN EYEBROW)

And how do we do that?

STEVE (DETERMINED)

I'll handle it at the station

tonight. We have access to various databases, and I should be able to identify the owner.

ALICE (PENSIVE)

Okay. While you do that, I'll head to the library. Maybe I can find old newspaper articles or documents about the clinic in the city archives.

STEVE (SMILING)

That sounds like a plan. The

library holds some very old, well-preserved records.

STEVE (SMILING) (CONT'D)

With a bit of luck, we might find some crucial leads there.

ALICE takes a sip of coffee, glances outside, then back at STEVE.

ALICE (WITH RENEWED COURAGE)

We can do this, right? We'll find

out what happened to Dennis and Tom.

STEVE (RESOLUTE)

Yes, Alice. We'll figure it out. It won't be easy, but we're on the right track.

ALICE (SOFT SMILE)

Thank you, Steve. For everything.

STEVE (GENTLY)

Don't mention it. We're a team, and teams stick together.

They sip their coffee and enjoy their pie, their eyes filled with determination. Despite all obstacles, they won't give up.

INT. POLICE STATION – HANK OBAMA'S OFFICE – DAY

The office of POLICE CHIEF HANK OBAMA (62) is modestly furnished. Medals and photographs from different stages of his career line the walls. He sits behind a heavy wooden desk, hands clasped, bearing the weight of an entire town.

Before him, MAYOR DONALD ABRAHAM (53) paces nervously. His face shows a mix-ture of worry and irritation. He represents the interests of local business owners who de-pend on tourism, and he has no patience for rumors or speculation about the rising num-ber of missing persons in the area. He's married and has a 17-year-old daughter.

MAYOR DONALD ABRAHAM (ANXIOUS)
Hank, the tourist season is just around the corner, and these
stories about missing people are spreading. It's going to ruin
our visitor numbers.

HANK OBAMA leans back, his gaze stern but calm.

HANK OBAMA (QUIETLY)

I understand, Donald, but people have the right
to know what's going on. We can't just sweep
this under the rug.

DONALD ABRAHAM stops abruptly, fixing Hank with an intense stare.

MAYOR DONALD ABRAHAM (SHARPLY)
I'm not saying we should ignore it. But word's out that Steve
is helping that woman, Alice, search for her son. That's
going to stir up too much dust—too much attention.

Hank sighs, rubbing his temples briefly.

HANK OBAMA (SOFTLY)

Steve's a good cop. He just wants to help.

MAYOR DONALD ABRAHAM   crosses his arms, voice growing more urgent.

MAYOR DONALD ABRAHAM

I don't care! We need to calm the situation, not create more chaos. Pull Steve back. Tell him to stay out of it.

Hank nods hesitantly, tension in his jaw.

HANK OBAMA (HEAVY-HEARTED)

I'll talk to him. But, Donald, the number of missing persons cases has risen sharply over the years. Our clearance rate is practically zero. We can't just ignore that.

DONALD ABRAHAM steps closer, voice firm.

MAYOR DONALD ABRAHAM

Make sure it's not our problem. The town needs a quiet season. No scandals, no missing persons reports. Fix it, Hank.

With that, he turns and leaves the office. The door closes softly behind him, leaving Hank alone, the weight of a difficult decision pressing down on his shoulders.

EXT. LIBRARY – DAY

The BLACK FORD RANGER pulls up in front of the library. ALICE (38) opens the door and steps out, her movements resolute. STEVE (42) remains in the driver's seat, watching her through the window.

STEVE (ENCOURAGING, WITH A SLIGHT SMILE)

Good luck, Alice. I'll let you know as soon as I find something.

ALICE nods, smiling back.

ALICE (GRATEFUL)

Thanks, Steve. We´ll stay in touch.

She closes the door and steps back as STEVE slowly turns the truck around. He gives her one last encouraging look before driving off. The FORD RANGER disappears into the distance.

ALICE stands there for a moment, watching him leave. Then she turns to face the LIBRARY. Her steps are firm and determined as she ascends the steps. The heavy wooden door opens with a quiet creak, and ALICE steps inside, ready to continue her search.

INT. LIBRARY – DAY

The library is quiet and peaceful, a welcome contrast to the gloomy atmosphere of the old clinic. ALICE (38) takes a deep breath, her determination growing as she approaches the RECEPTION DESK.

The LIBRARIAN (50s), polite but reserved, stands behind the counter. ALICE inquires about searching old newspapers. The librarian hands her a form, which ALICE begins to fill out.

LIBRARIAN (CURIOUS)

You're from London, right? What brings you here to
the town library as a tourist?

ALICE looks up from the form.

ALICE (SERIOUS)

I'm looking for my son Dennis and his friend Tom.
They've disappeared, and I have reason to believe
they were near that old psychiatric clinic.

ALICE (SERIOUS) (CONT'D)

I'm hoping to find something about the building's
past.

The librarian furrows her brow slightly, appearing sympathetic but also surprised.

LIBRARIAN (REGRETFUL) That clinic's been abandoned for decades. Oddly enough, most people in town don't seem very interested. I'm sorry, but I doubt you'll find any recent updates.

ALICE nods, taking the completed form.

ALICE (DETERMINED)

I understand. Still, I'll try

looking through old newspapers or archives.

The librarian offers a faint smile.

LIBRARIAN

Good luck. The archive computer is in the back corner. If you need any help, just let me know.

ALICE thanks her and walks past rows of shelves to the back corner of the room. She sits down at the computer, powers it up, and steels herself to delve into the town´s past in search of the truth.

INT. POLICE STATION – DAY

STEVE (42) enters the police station. A DESK OFFICER spots him immediately:

DESK OFFICER

Hey Steve, the chief wants to see you right away. He's not in a good mood.

STEVE raises an eyebrow, nodding curtly. He heads straight to the CHIEF'S OFFICE, where HANK OBAMA (62) waits impatiently behind his desk, brow furrowed.

STEVE closes the door and takes a seat.

STEVE (INQUIRING)
What's going on, Chief?

HANK OBAMA exhales heavily.

HANK OBAMA (IRRITATED)

The mayor was just here. Gave me an earful. It's about you helping that woman from London. He doesn't want any fuss, especially not with tourist season coming up.

STEVE lifts his hands calmly.

STEVE

I understand his concern, but people have been disappearing here for years. The numbers are way above average. Sooner or later, someone will notice. And what if there's a serial offender behind this? It can't hurt if I dig a little deeper, especially since I'm also helping her. Imagine if she goes to the press— that would be disastrous for the town.

HANK OBAMA's anger gives way to thoughtful consideration.

HANK OBAMA (RELENTING)

Fine. But do it quietly and preferably in your off-hours. Got it?

STEVE nods.

STEVE

Understood, Chief.

HANK OBAMA leans back, and the conversation ends. STEVE stands and leaves the office, heading to his own desk. There, he accesses a database and finds the current ca-retaker of the clinic: LOUIS BENSON, an attorney. STEVE jots down the address on a note.

A COLLEAGUE appears at his desk.

COLLEAGUE

Steve, come on, there's been a break-in at a warehouse!

STEVE tucks the note into his jacket pocket, grabs his coat, and follows his colleague outside.

INT. LIBRARY – DAY

ALICE (38) sits at an old COMPUTER in a quiet corner of the library.

She navigates through digital archives, clicking through pages as the screen flickers, slowly loading articles.

Old newspaper reports from the time of the clinic's closure appear on the monitor. Several headlines catch her eye:

ON SCREEN (newspaper clippings)

"MYSTERIOUS INCIDENTS AT THE CLINIC"

"UNEXPLAINED DEATHS AND DISAPPEARANCES"

"WHAT REALLY HAPPENED IN THE CLINIC?"

A PHOTO shows PROFESSOR LIVINGSTON, the former head of the clinic, pushing through a throng of REPORTERS. ALICE zooms in on his face, her gaze locked on the professor.

The articles mention unexplained deaths and disappearances at the former psychiatric clinic. ALICE jots down key dates, names, and facts in her NOTEBOOK: Professor Livingston… mysterious incidents… unexplained deaths…

ALICE takes out her PHONE and dials STEVE's number, pressing it to her ear. The phone rings, but no one answers. Eventually, the VOICEMAIL picks up.

ALICE (QUIETLY, URGENTLY)

Steve, I found something. Please call me back. Let's meet at the bar later.

Suddenly, the LIBRARIAN appears beside her, frowning.

LIBRARIAN (WHISPERING, DISPLEASED)

I'm sorry, but there's no phone use allowed in here. Please keep it down or step outside.

ALICE shrugs apologetically, closes her notebook, and stands up.

ALICE (WHISPERING)

I'm sorry. I'll leave now.

She exits the library quietly, her mind filled with new clues and questions. With Steve un-reachable, her worry increases, but so does her determination to uncover the truth about the clinic.

INT. ABANDONED PSYCHIATRIC CLINIC – ROOM – EVENING

In a dimly lit room, PAUL (24) and LUCY (19) have made themselves comfortable with their backpacks and sleeping bags. A small CAMPING LANTERN casts a warm glow, while soft music plays quietly from PAUL'S PHONE.

PAUL rolls a JOINT, lights it, and takes a long, deep drag. He holds the smoke briefly before exhaling with satisfaction, then passes it to LUCY, who also takes a hit.

PAUL (RELAXED, SLIGHTLY MOCKING)

Those warnings from that Alice woman and the cop? Ridicu-lous. It's totally chill here. We can easily stay a few days, no problem.

LUCY, now slightly buzzed, nods and smiles dreamily.

LUCY (SMIRKING)

Maybe this really is a hidden gem. Doesn't sound so bad at all. Maybe we'll be lucky and this is a real insider tip. If we stay here for a few more days, we'll have enough time to shoot some videos for our blog.

PAUL lies back, arms folded behind his head, while LUCY settles in beside him. The music, the soft lantern light, and the sweet scent of the joint combine to create an almost idyllic atmosphere.

They seem to have pushed aside all the grim rumors about the clinic, choosing instead to bask in the moment, drifting into a state of deceptive calm and comfort.

INT. BAR – EVENING

ALICE (38) sits at a window table, her NOTES spread out before her, a GLASS OF RED WINE at her side. The bar is not very crowded tonight. A few MEN play pool and chat, while a handful of PATRONS at the bar sip their last drinks of the evening.

ALICE flips through her notes when the DOOR opens and STEVE (42) enters. He takes a quick look around, nods to some familiar FACES and the BARTENDER, then heads straight toward ALICE.

                    STEVE (FRIENDLY, SOFTLY)

          Hey, Alice. There you are.

ALICE looks up, relieved.

                              ALICE

          Hey, Steve. Glad you could make it.

STEVE takes a seat and leans in slightly.

                         STEVE (SERIOUS)

          So, what did you find out?

ALICE takes a sip of her wine, gathering her thoughts.

                      ALICE (QUIET, INTENT)

              I went through old newspaper articles at the
              library. There were unexplained deaths, missing
              people... and this Professor Livingston, the for-
              mer head of the clinic, was at the center of it all.
              Everything suggests something very disturbing
              happened there.

STEVE's brow furrows.

                              STEVE

              Professor Livingston, huh? Interesting. I have news
              too. The chief gave me a hard time because the
              mayor's on edge, but I'm allowed to continue as
              long as I keep things low-key. Plus, I found out who
              manages the clinic now—an attorney named Louis
              Benson.

ALICE makes a note.

ALICE

Louis Benson… he might have records, land deeds,
patient files, or staff records. Something that can
help us piece this together.

STEVE nods in agreement.

STEVE

Exactly what I thought. We should visit him tomorrow morning. Maybe he has documents that will
help us solve this puzzle.

ALICE places her hand briefly on Steve's forearm, her expression tense.

ALICE (UNCERTAIN)

I'm scared, Steve. At first, I just wanted to find Dennis
and Tom, but ever since we were inside that clinic,
I've had this horrible feeling. Something's there… I
can't explain it, but it won't leave me.

STEVE gently covers her hand with his.

STEVE (REASSURING)

I understand your fear. But we'll face this together.
I'll stand by you as long as you need me.

ALICE feels the warmth of his hand, then gently withdraws her own, offering a grateful
smile.

ALICE (SOFTLY)

Thank you, Steve. It means a lot.

For a moment, they enjoy this brief reprieve. The world outside fades, leaving them sitting together under the bar's warm glow, united in their resolve to face whatever comes
next.

INT. HOTEL ROOM – NIGHT

ALICE (38) lies asleep in her HOTEL BED. The room is dark, faint streetlight filtering
through the curtains. The CAMERA slowly moves toward her face. Her closed EYES

42

dart beneath the lids, indicating a vivid dream.

DREAM SEQUENCE:

INT. ABANDONED PSYCHIATRIC CLINIC – HALLWAY – TIME UNKNOWN

We are in a long, dimly lit HALLWAY of the abandoned clinic. DENNIS (20) stands several meters ahead, facing the camera. The hallway is silent and eerie, but Dennis initially appears calm.

>   DENNIS (QUIETLY, REASSURING) Don't
> worry, I'm fine. We've found something truly amazing
> here.

The CAMERA moves closer to DENNIS as he turns away, looking toward the end of the hallway, and continues speaking in a hushed, almost excited tone.

>   DENNIS (SOFTLY, ALMOST WHISPERING) (CONT'D)
>
> It's so beautiful. And if you stay very still and lis-
> ten closely, you can hear it. Pssssst, hush… do
> you hear it?

The CAMERA is now directly behind DENNIS. Suddenly, he whips back around, facing the CAMERA. His FACE contorts into a hideous, demonic grimace, hollow, grey eyes staring emptily. His VOICE becomes deep, distorted, and menacing.

>   DENNIS (DISTORTED VOICE) (CONT'D)
>
> Can you hear it now, Alice?!

BACK TO REALITY:

ALICE jolts awake, breathing heavily, sweat on her brow. She sits up in bed, heart pounding. With trembling hands she covers her face, tears streaming down her cheeks. She weeps softly in the darkness, still shaken by the nightmare.

INT. LOUIS BENSON'S LAW OFFICE – DAY

ALICE (38) and STEVE (42) sit before the desk of LOUIS BENSON (38), a nervous, scattered attorney. A nameplate on the sturdy wooden DESK reads "Louis Benson / Attorney." Behind him, a large WINDOW lets in light, while shelves of BOOKS, CER-TIFICATES, and AWARDS line the walls.

BENSON rifles through FILES, repeatedly pushing his small, round GLASSES up his nose, making a pinched expression each time.

> BENSON (FIDGETY)
> As I mentioned, I'm just responsible
> for the usual
>
> procedures: taxes, fees, insurance. Mostly, I fend
> off pesky brokers and investors who'd love to turn
> the property into a hotel. But that, he raises a fin-
> ger, will never happen according to my predeces-
> sor and principal.

ALICE and STEVE exchange a frustrated glance. BENSON shrugs, pushing his glasses up again.

> BENSON (HESITANT) (CONT'D)
>
> I took over the firm a few years ago. I know al-
> most nothing about the clinic itself or the owner.
> I never questioned it.

> BENSON (HESITANT) (CONT'D)
>
> The fees come in regularly and form the bulk of my
> income. That's it. I can't give you much more.

STEVE nods, disappointed.

> STEVE
>
> What about the owner's address?

BENSON pulls out a file, flips through a few pages, adjusts his glasses once more, and extracts a piece of paper.

> BENSON (MATTER-OF-FACT)
>
> Here. Professor Livingston. This is the official
> contact address. That's all I can provide.

ALICE takes the slip of paper, shares a meaningful look with STEVE. Both stand up.

ALICE (POLITELY)

Thank you, Mr. Benson. We appreciate your help.

BENSON waves a hand dismissively, glasses slipping again, as they turn to leave.

BENSON (CALLING AFTER THEM)

And just so we're clear! The clinic   is absolutely not for
sale!

STEVE and ALICE pause, exchange a glance, then continue down the hallway. Their
footsteps echo as they mentally follow this new lead—Professor Livingston—into unknown territory.

EXT. OUTSIDE THE LAWYER'S OFFICE – DAY

STEVE's car remains parked outside the lawyer's building. Inside, STEVE (42) sits
behind the wheel and ALICE (38) in the passenger seat. The tension is palpable as
they process the new information. ALICE holds the slip of paper with Professor
Livingston's address.

ALICE (THOUGHTFUL)

Steve, in the newspaper photo, the professor looked
at least sixty thirty years ago. He'd have to be long
dead by now.

STEVE glances at her reassuringly.

STEVE (CALMLY)

You might be right, Alice. But think about it: the
lawyer still gets paid. Someone is behind this, someone who might be able to help us. We finally
have a lead, and we should follow it. Whether the
professor is still alive or not, this address could lead
us to someone who knows more.

ALICE takes a deep breath and nods.

ALICE (DETERMINED)

You're right. This is our best chance to learn more
about the clinic and the disappearance of the boys.
Let's go.

STEVE starts the engine and carefully pulls the car onto the road. ALICE casts one last glance at the office building before turning forward again.

Outside, the scenery blurs as the car gains speed. Inside, the mood is grave but full of resolve. STEVE heads toward the city limits, ready to dig deeper into the mystery.

INT. MAYOR DONALD ABRAHAM'S OFFICE – DAY

A somewhat opulent office. MAYOR DONALD ABRAHAM (53) sits behind a massive DESK, speaking tersely on the PHONE. He sounds irritated.

> MAYOR DONALD ABRAHAM (IMPATIENT, INTO PHONE)
>
> I've told you a thousand times: with tourist season starting, we can't afford any bad news! Sort it out. Now!

He slams the RECEIVER down, exhales in frustration, muttering under his breath. The SECRETARY (40s) enters carrying a FOLDER, placing it before him for SIGNATURE.

> SECRETARY (CAUTIOUSLY)
>
> Mr. Mayor, here's the file for the new construction project. Also, your daughter AMELIA ABRAHAM's waiting in my office.

The MAYOR DONALD ABRAHAM picks up a PEN and signs the documents. Hearing AMELIA ABRAHAM's name, he looks up briefly.

> MAYOR DONALD ABRAHAM (CURT BUT MEASURED)
>
> Send her in.

The SECRETARY closes the FOLDER, nods, and exits. Moments later, AMELIA ABRAHAM (17) enters, taking a seat in front of the DESK. The SECRETARY shuts the DOOR behind her.

> MAYOR DONALD ABRAHAM (IRRITABLE)(CONT'D)
>
> Yes, AMELIA ABRAHAM? What is it?

AMELIA ABRAHAM folds her arms, visibly upset but trying to remain composed.

                    AMELIA ABRAHAM (DEFIANT)

         I just wanted to remind you that my birthday is this
         weekend. You promised to organize the party for me.

The MAYOR DONALD ABRAHAM sighs, rubbing his temples.

                    MAYOR DONALD ABRAHAM (STRESSED)
         AMELIA ABRAHAM, now's not a good time. I'm under mas-
         sive pressure because of these… incidents. Tourist season is
         starting, and we can't handle any more trouble.

AMELIA ABRAHAM raises her chin, her voice growing louder.

                    AMELIA ABRAHAM (INDIGNANT)

         I don't care! You promised. You   can't just cancel or
         postpone. It's my birthday!

The MAYOR DONALD ABRAHAM puts the papers aside, trying to keep his cool.

                    MAYOR DONALD ABRAHAM (PLACATING)
         Look, I'm only postponing the party

         a bit. If we do it later, we'll do it big—with all the
         bells and whistles. Okay?

AMELIA ABRAHAM jumps to her feet, anger clear in her expression.

                    AMELIA ABRAHAM (ANGRY)

          No, that's not okay! I want to celebrate on my ac-
         tual birthday, not some random date. You always
         put your job first and never think about me!

The MAYOR DONALD ABRAHAM opens his mouth to respond, but AMELIA AB-
RAHAM rushes to the DOOR.

                    AMELIA ABRAHAM (FURIOUS)(CONT'D)

         Forget it! I´ll handle it myself.

She storms out, slamming the DOOR. The MAYOR DONALD ABRAHAM remains a-
lone, even more irritated than before. He stares at the now-closed FILES, as the echo
of the door slam fades in the reception area.

INT. STEVE'S CAR – DAY

STEVE (42) has parked his FORD RANGER in front of an old yet well-maintained
HOUSE on the outskirts of town. Through the windshield, the building is clearly visible.
ALICE (38) sits in the passenger seat, holding a NOTE with an address.

> ALICE (DOUBTFUL)
>
> According to the lawyer, this is Professor Livings-
> ton's address. (hesitates)

He'd be in his nineties by now… or maybe not alive at all.

STEVE glances at the house, then at ALICE.

> STEVE (REASSURING)
>
> That's possible. But as long as the lawyer keeps
> getting paid, someone has to be behind this.
>
> (gestures to the house) Let's find
> out.

ALICE exhales, still holding the NOTE.

> ALICE (RESOLUTE)
>
> This might be our best lead to
>
> learn more about the clinic – and about Dennis
> and Tom.

STEVE nods, turns off the engine, and both step out.

EXT. HOUSE ON THE OUTSKIRTS – DAY

A small, tidy FRONT YARD leads to the old HOUSE. ALICE and STEVE walk along the
narrow PATH toward the front door. ALICE holds the NOTE, looking tense.

ALICE (QUIETLY)

I really hope we find some answers here.

STEVE (ENCOURAGING)   We'll see.
At least we can clear up a few open questions.

STEVE knocks firmly on the door. After a brief moment, it opens slowly, revealing DANIEL LIVINGSTON (72) eyeing them warily.

DANIEL (GRUFFLY)

Yes?

ALICE looks to STEVE, who now takes the NOTE from her and keeps it in his hand.

STEVE (POLITE BUT FIRM)

Good day. My name is Steve Miles, and this is
Alice Walker. We're looking for Mr. Livingston.

DANIEL folds his arms.

DANIEL

I'm Mr. Livingston. What do you want?

ALICE and STEVE exchange a surprised glance—they expected someone much older or perhaps no one at all.

ALICE (ASTONISHED)

We... well, we've seen old photographs of
Professor Livingston. He looked quite
elderly even decades ago. We honestly
didn't think—

DANIEL gives a short, dry laugh.

DANIEL

Then you're talking about my father, Theodor
Livingston. He was the one who ran the clinic back
then.

                              (raises an eyebrow) What do you
          want from him?

STEVE glances down at the NOTE in his hand, as if double-checking it, then slips it
into his JACKET POCKET and speaks calmly.

                              STEVE (CALMLY)

          We're looking for information about the old psychiat-
          ric clinic.

                              STEVE (CALMLY) (CONT'D)

          Lawyer Louis Benson gave us this address, thin-
          king you or your father might be able to help.

DANIEL seems to relax slightly, apparently relieved they're not buyers.

                              DANIEL

          So you're not real estate agents wanting to tear it
          all down.

ALICE shakes her head.

                              ALICE

          No, we're not trying to purchase anything. My son is
          missing, and we suspect the clinic may be involved.
          We need its history.

DANIEL looks them over again, then nods slowly.

                              DANIEL

          I see. All right. Come in. Maybe I can help.

He opens the door wider. ALICE and STEVE step inside as DANIEL closes it behind
them. The dimly lit HALLWAY is lined with old photographs, and the soft creaking of
floorboards intensifies the tension—answers or fresh mysteries may lie ahead.

INT. LIVING ROOM – DAY

A cozy, somewhat old-fashioned PARLOR. ALICE (38) and STEVE (42) sit on an old
COUCH. In front of them is a low TABLE with two GLASSES. DANIEL (72) enters
from the adjacent KITCHEN, carrying a PITCHER of water.

DANIEL sets the pitcher down and pours water for ALICE and STEVE.

DANIEL (REGRETFUL)

I'm truly sorry about those boys, but I'm afraid I can't
help. When the clinic closed, I was living in Glasgow
and hardly in touch with my father. Things only changed after it was already shut down and he needed
my help.

ALICE glances at STEVE, disappointment on her face. They each hold their GLASS but
barely drink.

ALICE (DESPONDENT)

We've run out of leads. All I have is this clinic and
a few vague hints…

STEVE (THOUGHTFUL)

We were hoping to learn something new here. Any
clue that might help us move forward.

DANIEL sighs and gestures apologetically.

DANIEL

I understand your situation, but I really don't know
what else I can offer. My father hardly spoke about
the clinic. I only reconnected with him well after it was
closed.

Suddenly, a THUMPING noise comes from the FLOOR ABOVE. ALICE and STEVE
start, exchanging puzzled looks. DANIEL, however, stands calmly, seemingly unsurpri-
sed.

DANIEL (CASUALLY) (CONT'D)

Ah, that's probably the professor. Sounds like he
just woke up. Maybe you can ask him yourselves.

ALICE and STEVE stare at him in astonishment, then exchange a hopeful glance. Both
rise from the COUCH as DANIEL heads toward the STAIRS.

ALICE (RELIEVED, CONFUSED)

The professor…? He's… really still alive here?

STEVE (QUIETLY, EXCITED)

This is our chance…

DANIEL raises an eyebrow, a slight smile tugging at his lips.

DANIEL

Well, come on then. He might tell you more than
he's ever told me.

ALICE and STEVE follow DANIEL, who's already waiting at the STAIRS. With mingled feelings of hope and confusion, they trail behind him as the thumping noise above grows louder.

INT. UPPER FLOOR ROOM – DAY

An old, dimly lit ROOM. A curtain filters the daylight, bathing everything in half-darkness.

The PROFESSOR (90+) sits in an antique WHEELCHAIR near the WINDOW, his BACK turned to the door. His bony HANDS rest on the armrests, his shoulders slumped.

DANIEL (72) enters with ALICE (38) and STEVE (42). ALICE and STEVE linger near the DOOR, while DANIEL approaches his father.

PROFESSOR (TREMULOUS VOICE, NOT TURNING AROUND)

Daniel…? Who's there?

DANIEL glances at ALICE and STEVE.

DANIEL (SOFTLY)

Father, this is Alice and Steve. They'd like to
talk to you about

the clinic. But if you don't want—

The PROFESSOR groans, his left arm twitching slightly. He breathes heavily, as if trying to gather himself.

PROFESSOR (PENSIVELY, WITH PAUSES)

The clinic… yes…

(pause, brief trembling) So many rumors… just rumors.

DANIEL turns to ALICE and STEVE, gesturing for them to come closer. They do so, cautiously observing the ancient figure barely visible in the half-light.

ALICE (CAREFUL)

Professor, we… we've heard you once ran the clinic. In recent years, an unusually high number of people have gone missing in this area. One of them is my son, Dennis. We suspect there might be a connection to the clinic.

The PROFESSOR twitches his right fingers as if trying to grasp something. After a short, labored breath, he lifts his hand, beckoning them closer.

PROFESSOR (FRAIL VOICE)

Missing…

(pause, lost in thought) There were always… rumors about vanishing patients.

(pause) Incompetent staff…

(breath falters, he coughs)

PROFESSOR (FRAIL VOICE) (CONT'D)

…and corruption… yes, corruption everywhere.

STEVE steps forward, wanting to help the PROFESSOR, but DANIEL holds him back momentarily.

STEVE (CALMLY)

Sir, please understand we're not here to cause trouble. I'm Steve Miles, a police officer, and Alice is the

mother of a missing young man. We have no other
leads—your clinic is our only clue.

The PROFESSOR lowers one hand onto the armrest, exhaling shakily. His voice
shifts between clarity and a vague, distant emptiness.

PROFESSOR (DISTANT)

Missing…

(pause, seeming to lose himself in
memories)

No. Not missing… they were… (pause,
stares blankly)

…set free… yes, set free.

ALICE glances at STEVE, confused. She steps closer, her tone gentle.

ALICE (SOFTLY)

Professor, you have to understand—we're desperate. Dennis has been gone for weeks. Many people have disappeared around here over the past few years. Some say
there are dark secrets in the clinic, hidden rooms… experiments.

Suddenly, the PROFESSOR breathes louder, his shoulders tense. His voice rises in agi-
tation.

PROFESSOR (AGITATED, WITH PAUSES)

Experiments… incompetent staff…

They ruined everything! (pause, jaw trembling)

People talk. They spread lies. (pause, struggling to

focus)

They believe… whatever they want.

DANIEL places a reassuring hand on his father's shoulder. The PROFESSOR swallows,
as if battling fragments of memories or trying to piece them together.

DANIEL (GENTLE)

Father, you don't have to force yourself. Alice

and Steve only want—

Without warning, the PROFESSOR seizes ALICE'S HAND which is near the wheelchair. He grips it astonishingly hard, causing ALICE to gasp in pain and lean down to his level. The PROFESSOR's hollow, lifeless EYES lock onto hers.

> PROFESSOR (HOARSE, GRAVE)
> Leave the past buried…
>
> (pause, gaze chillingly detached)
>
> …or you will never find peace.

ALICE wrenches free, stumbling back. At once, the PROFESSOR starts convulsing, trembling violently in his WHEELCHAIR. His BONY HANDS clutch the armrests, nearly splintering them, and he thrashes his head side to side, emitting ragged sounds.

DANIEL rushes forward, trying to calm his father, retrieving a SYRINGE from his pocket. He injects it into the PROFESSOR's upper arm.

> DANIEL (URGENT, TO ALICE AND STEVE)
> Please leave. It's too much for him—he's having an episode. Wait downstairs for me!

ALICE and STEVE hesitate, then hurry toward the DOOR. Before ALICE leaves, she glances back. At that instant, the PROFESSOR whips his head around, eyes wide, the IRISES black as ink. ALICE recoils in horror.

DANIEL pushes them out, shutting the DOOR behind them with a resounding THUD that echoes in the hallway, leaving the muffled sounds of the PROFESSOR´s spasms behind.

INT. LIVING ROOM – DAY

ALICE (38) and STEVE (42) descend the STAIRS, visibly shaken by their encounter with the PROFESSOR. Faint groans and noises can still be heard from UPSTAIRS.

> ALICE (QUIET, UPSET)
> Did you see his eyes, Steve? That wasn't normal.
> I've never seen anything like that.

STEVE nods, furrowing his brow.

STEVE (SOFTLY)

Yeah, I saw. I'm not sure what that was, but it's definitely not normal. Could be some effect of his condition, or…

He trails off as DANIEL (72) enters the LIVING ROOM, hands clasped nervously.

DANIEL (APOLOGETIC)

I'm so sorry about my father. He sometimes has
these episodes, but never as intense as this one.

ALICE glances at STEVE, taking a steadying breath. STEVE just nods.

DANIEL moves to a CABINET, opens it, and removes a FOLDER. He sets it on the
TABLE and sorts through some papers. Finally, he takes out a single sheet and writes
something down on a small NOTE.

DANIEL (CALMLY)(CONT'D)

Listen, a few years back, a former nurse got in
touch with me—Doris Evens. She's around sixty
now. She used to work for my father at the clinic,
before it closed.

(hands ALICE the note)   Here's her
address. Maybe she can tell you more.

ALICE takes the slip of paper, studying the address.

ALICE (HOPEFUL)

Thank you. This could really help us.

DANIEL closes the FOLDER and returns it to the cabinet. He casts a restless look at
ALICE and STEVE, eager to usher them out.

DANIEL (CURT)

I think you should go now. My father needs rest. I…
hope you find what you're looking for.

ALICE and STEVE nod, still unsettled.

STEVE (POLITELY)

We appreciate your help. Please let your father know
we won't bother him again.

DANIEL already holds the FRONT DOOR open, nodding briefly.

DANIEL

Take care.

ALICE and STEVE step out onto the PORCH as DANIEL swiftly shuts the door behind them. ALICE throws one last look over her shoulder, then they descend the steps
and leave the property.

INT. PROFESSOR'S ROOM – DAY

The PROFESSOR (90+) sits in his antiquated WHEELCHAIR, the room dimly lit. It
appears that his recent seizure has subsided. His EYELIDS are closed, but behind
them, his EYEBALLS twitch restlessly, as if he's trapped in a disturbing dream.

Suddenly, he snaps his EYES open. The IRISES are completely black, dark, throbbing
VEINS emerging around his eye sockets. His bony HANDS grip the WHEELCHAIR'S
armrests with renewed ferocity, and his entire BODY begins convulsing again.

He emits a low, tormented GROAN, followed by strange, indecipherable SOUNDS, as
if speaking in an unknown tongue. The scene ends on the image of the PROFESSOR,
once more locked in a violent episode that leaves him hovering between madness and
reality.

INT. ABANDONED PSYCHIATRIC CLINIC – ROOM – NIGHT

A dark, forsaken ROOM. LUCY (19) and PAUL (24) have unrolled their SLEEPING
MATS, half-covered by a BLANKET. Their breathing is heavy as they make passionate
love. A small CAMPING LANTERN casts faint light. Low MUSIC plays from a SPEA-
KER.

In a rusty TIN, a nearly burnt-out JOINT still smolders. Despite their intimate moment, the setting is

oppressive—chipped walls, rotten debris, and the musty smell of decay.

As soft music and the sounds of their passion fill the space, strange NOISES and a low,
incomprehensible MURMUR begin to overlay them. LUCY's eyes snap open, listening

intently.

LUCY (QUIET, UNEASY)

Paul, do you hear that? There's… something…

PAUL (BREATHLESS, ABSORBED)
Shhh… Lucy, don't worry…

(he kisses her neck ardently)

LUCY tries to focus, but her gaze drifts to the CEI-
LING. Within the lantern's glow, she sees BLACK
VEINS spreading, inch by inch, as though alive.

LUCY (NOW TERRIFIED)

Paul, please! Look up there!

PAUL (ANNOYED)
Lucy, come on, what—

He briefly lifts his head, but LUCY starts screaming in panic. The BLACK VEINS on
the ceiling seem to writhe and pulsate. Just as PAUL is about to speak, an invisible
FORCE grabs him by the FEET, dragging him away from LUCY into the DARKNESS.

The last thing LUCY sees of him is PAUL'S desperate FACE, eyes wide and turning black.

LUCY (SCREAMING)
PAUL!

She pushes herself back with her FEET, pulling free from the BLANKET. With a frantic
cry, she scrambles to the DOOR, fleeing into the pitch-black HALLWAY.

INT. HALLWAY – CONTINUOUS – NIGHT

Only the flicker of the CAMPING LANTERN remains visible for a split second before it
goes out, and the MUSIC abruptly stops. LUCY sprints down the corridor as fast as she
can, repeatedly bumping into DOOR FRAMES and peeling WALLS. Her breathing is
ragged while the eerie NOISES and that ominous MURMURING VOICE grow louder behind her.

The ROOM she was just in is now in total darkness. A brief final flicker of the lantern illuminates shapes on the walls, then everything plunges into black. LUCY screams again, stumbling through the long corridors—desperate to escape the horror closing in behind her.

INT. PROFESSOR'S ROOM – DAY

The PROFESSOR (90+) remains in his old WHEELCHAIR. The violent convulsions that racked his body moments ago gradually subside.

His bony HANDS loosen their grip on the armrests, and the dark VEINS across his TEMPLES and around his EYES slowly fade.

For a brief moment, his body is still wracked by one last tremor before falling limp. The PROFESSOR inhales shakily, then slowly opens his EYES. They are once again normal in color.

                    PROFESSOR (SOFT, EXHAUSTED)
          Ha…

               (a trembling breath) …it's over…

Relief washes over him, yet he appears utterly drained. He leans back wearily, letting his head loll to the side as if on the verge of drifting into a profound sleep. The silence in the room underscores that he seems to have escaped some dark influence or terrifying state—at least for now—though he's left spent and utterly exhausted.

INT./EXT. STEVE'S CAR – DAY

STEVE (42)'s FORD RANGER remains parked in front of the PROFESSOR's old yet well-maintained HOUSE. ALICE (38) and STEVE sit inside the vehicle, still rattled by recent events.

                    ALICE (THOUGHTFUL)

          Steve, I'm certain the professor isn't telling us the
          whole truth. His behavior, those outbursts… I think
          he's hiding something about the clinic.

                    STEVE (AGREEING)

          I feel the same way. Something's off. Do you still
          have that note Daniel gave you?

ALICE hands STEVE the note with the former nurse's address.

> ### STEVE (CONSIDERING) (CONT'D)
>
> Doris Evens… Let me see if I can get her number.

He picks up his phone and dials a colleague at the station.

> ### STEVE (INTO PHONE) (CONT'D)
>
> Hey, Miles here. Could you look up a number for me? A Doris Evens, used to work at the old clinic… Yeah, that's right.

> ### STEVE (INTO PHONE) (CONT'D)
>
> (pause while he listens) Great, thanks.

STEVE jots down the number, glances briefly at ALICE.

> ### STEVE (QUIETLY, TO ALICE) (CONT'D)
>
> I'll call her right now.

He inputs the number and waits as it rings.

> ### STEVE (INTO PHONE) (CONT'D)
>
> Hello, this is Steve Miles from the Pearl Harbor police. I got your address from… Yes, Doris Evens? I'd like to speak with you briefly about the old clinic—it's related to an ongoing case…
>
> (short pause, he nods)
>
> I see. Could we come by? It's quite urgent.
>
> (smiles, nods again) Great, thanks.
> We'll be right there.

He hangs up, turning to ALICE with a small, relieved grin.

> ### STEVE (RELIEVED) (CONT'D)
>
> She lives on our way back into town and can see us right now. We can head over immediately.

ALICE breathes a sigh of relief, gratitude and determination in her eyes.

ALICE (SINCERELY)

Thank you, Steve. I'd be totally lost without you.

STEVE returns a brief smile and starts the ENGINE. With one last look at the PROFES-
SOR's HOUSE, where they just witnessed something inexplicable, he eases the CAR
onto the road. ALICE also glances back, and then they drive away, following a new lead
that might finally give them answers.

INT. ABANDONED PSYCHIATRIC CLINIC – HALLWAY – NIGHT

LUCY (19) tears through the dark CORRIDOR, screaming at the top of her lungs. Her
feet slip on the dusty floor, and she brushes repeatedly against damp, crumbling
walls. Haunting NOISES trail her—an ominous whisper, a scraping sound that feels
unbearably close.

Suddenly, the CORRIDOR opens into the deserted, spacious LOBBY. The massive DOOR to the outside stands half ajar, allowing a faint glimmer from outside
to spill in.

LUCY (PANICKED, BREATHLESS)

Oh god… got to get out…

With her last ounce of strength, she sprints across the hall's debris-strewn floor, nearly
tripping over broken tiles. Shadows behind her seem to stretch forward, as if the un-
seen FORCE is reaching for her.

EXT. ABANDONED PSYCHIATRIC CLINIC – OUTSIDE / EDGE OF THE
WOODS – NIGHT

The moment LUCY bursts through the half-open DOOR into the night air, the terrifying
sounds abruptly cease. No more whispers, no more scratching. Only her ragged breathing and the crisp night air remain.

She stumbles onward, away from the building, eyes wide with terror. She doesn't look
back, determined only to flee. The WOODLAND ahead looms in her path.

LUCY (DESPERATE)
No… just away… get away…

Without slowing, she plunges into the undergrowth, flinging aside branches that whip
at her face. Her FEET tangle with roots and thorns, carrying her deeper into the

darkness of the forest -- anything to escape the horror of the clinic behind her.

INT. DORIS' APARTMENT – EVENING

A cozy LIVING ROOM. A low TABLE in the center holds half-filled GLASSES and a VASE of fresh flowers. ALICE (38) and STEVE (42) sit together on a COUCH, while DORIS EVENS (60) sits across from them in an armchair.

STEVE (POLITELY)

Thank you for seeing us so late, Doris. We really didn't mean to ambush you, but it's urgent.

DORIS raises a reassuring hand, offering a gentle smile.

DORIS

It's no trouble. I've got plenty of free time these days. And you sounded like it couldn't wait.

STEVE exhales, taking a sip from his glass.

STEVE (CALM)

We visited Professor Livingston today—Alice and I. He's… not well. We'd hoped to learn something about the clinic, but the meeting was extremely odd.

ALICE glances at STEVE briefly, then addresses DORIS.

ALICE (RESIGNED)

I'm searching for my son Dennis and his friend Tom. They've vanished. And somehow, every lead, every clue, leads back to the clinic. But no one can give us a straight answer. I… I'm at a loss.

DORIS leans forward, sensing ALICE's desperation. She picks up her glasses, sets them down again, and clears her throat.

DORIS (GENTLE, EMPATHETIC)

Oh dear, I'm so sorry. I know the rumors about the clinic—folks around here don't like talking about it at all.

She hesitates for a moment, as though gathering courage.

                    DORIS (SOFTLY) (CONT'D)

        I started working there right after my nurse training. I
        was young, inexperienced, but excited. At first, every-
        thing was great. We had a friendly team, and the pro-
        fessor was so charismatic. I really enjoyed my job.

ALICE leans in, STEVE takes another sip from his glass. Both are transfixed.

                    ALICE (CAUTIOUSLY)

        What happened then?

DORIS sighs, letting her gaze roam around the room like she's recalling something unsettling.

                    DORIS (HUSHED)

        It all changed when they admitted a patient—Alexan-
        der O'Kelly. From that day on, nothing was the
        same.

ALICE and STEVE exchange a quick, alarmed glance. DORIS appears visibly moved, but presses on in a quieter voice.

                    DORIS (WHISPERING) (CONT'D)

        I can still see it in my mind: the moment he arrived.
        His eyes… the look on his face. Even then, I felt so-
        mething dark about him…

She falls silent, eyes drifting to the half-filled GLASSES on the table. ALICE and STEVE
sit in tense anticipation, waiting to learn more about Alexander O'Kelly and whatever
dark secrets might lie behind his name.

INT. PSYCHIATRIC CLINIC – RECEPTION AREA – DAY (FLASHBACK)

DORIS (25) stands behind the reception desk. An OLDER NURSE beside her is focused
on writing a report. Two ORDERLIES haul in a violently struggling ALEXANDER
O'KELLY (in a STRAITJACKET). O'KELLY shouts, curses, and fights against them with
all his might.

O'KELLY (ANGRY, LOUD)

Let me go! You're the crazy ones, not me!

The ORDERLIES pin him to the wall near the desk while the OLDER NURSE begins the intake process. DORIS looks on, horrified by this newcomer.

DORIS (V.O.)

"I remember that day so well, when Alexander O'Kelly was admitted. He wasn't a typical patient. You could feel an overwhelming rage emanating from him, more intense than anything I'd seen before. But that was only the beginning…"

INT. PSYCHIATRIC CLINIC - PROFESSOR'S OFFICE – DAY (FLASH-BACK)

O'KELLY, arms confined by the STRAITJACKET, is seated on a CHAIR. Two ORDER-LIES stand watch. PROFESSOR LIVINGSTON, then in his mid-60s, studies the patient intently. DORIS stands beside the professor, taking notes, visibly uneasy as O'KELLY rants and raves.

O'KELLY (MENACING)
You're all going to see what happens!

The PROFESSOR remains composed, quietly instructing one of the ORDERLIES. DO-RIS jots down details with a trembling hand.

DORIS (V.O.)

"Back then, Professor Livingston appeared to be capable of handling anything. I was young and im-pressed, even as O'Kelly's presence unsettled me. Still, I hoped the professor had everything under control…"

INT. PSYCHIATRIC CLINIC – O'KELLY'S ROOM – DAY (FLASHBACK)

A NURSE briefly opens the DOOR; DORIS glances inside before the door is shut again. O'KELLY sits sedated on his BED, still wearing the STRAITJACKET, eyes wide open, wearing a disturbing GRIN. DORIS freezes in fright.

                              DORIS (V.O.)

        "Initially, I thought he was just an exceptionally difficult
        case. But from the moment O'Kelly arrived, the atmosphere
        in the entire clinic began to change. I couldn't put my finger
        on it, but it was as if he brought something dark with him…"

INT. PSYCHIATRIC CLINIC – HALLWAY / EMPTY PATIENT ROOM – DAY (FLASH-
BACK)

A PATIENT ROOM lies EMPTY; the BED untouched, the patient missing. DORIS, the
PROFESSOR, and several ORDERLIES stand in the hallway, stunned.

                          ORDERLY 1 (IN DISBELIEF)

        I was just here a few minutes ago… How could he vanish
        like that?

                      PROFESSOR (QUIETLY, SHOCKED)

        This is impossible…

DORIS looks on, horrified. Confusion and dread are palpable among them.

                              DORIS (V.O.)

        "And he wasn't the only one who disappeared. No,
        O'Kelly remained, but after his arrival, more and
        more patients simply vanished without a trace. I still
        don't know what darkness he brought with him, but
        the clinic was never the same again…"

The scene fades as DORIS, the PROFESSOR, and the ORDERLIES stare into the
empty room where the patient has inexplicably gone missing.

INT. DORIS' APARTMENT – EVENING

ALICE (38) and STEVE (42) remain seated with DORIS (60) in her cozy living room, gathered around the small COFFEE TABLE. Their glasses are nearly empty. Tension and
relief intertwine, as DORIS has just recounted her experiences at the old clinic.

                      DORIS (QUIETLY, PENSIVELY)

                                  65

After that point, the clinic just kept spiraling down-
ward. People went missing—first patients, then even
nurses and orderlies… The rumors around town grew
wilder. Eventually, the clinic was shut down for good.

ALICE and STEVE listen closely, equal parts fascinated and unnerved.

DORIS (SIGHING) (CONT'D)

It all became too frightening for me. I was still young
and found another job. Later on, I only read in the papers about everything that happened. I was so relieved I wasn't there anymore. Who knows what might
have become of me otherwise…

ALICE (SYMPATHETIC)

That must have been terrifying.

DORIS nods, looking down at her hands.

DORIS (CALMLY)

I never imagined the professor would live so long. A
few years ago, I heard he was still alive, so I contac-
ted his son. But we never actually met—he was un-
well at the time, and the contact just fizzled out.

(raising her gaze)

Honestly, I'm glad it didn't work out. Those horrible
images in my mind… that uneasy feeling never really
left me. I've lived my life, but… I feel better for sha-
ring it now. And if it helps you, all the better.

ALICE and STEVE share a grateful glance.

STEVE (GRATEFUL)

Doris, you've been a tremendous help. We really appreciate it.

ALICE (WARMLY)

Thank you so much. It can't have been easy for you
to relive it all.

DORIS smiles gently, stands, and leads ALICE and STEVE to the door.

DORIS

Please take care of yourselves. I hope you find
what you're looking for.

ALICE and STEVE bid her a heartfelt farewell, clearly moved by her accounts. They
step out into the hallway.

EXT. FOREST – NIGHT

LUCY (19) wanders through the dark woods, wearing only minimal clothing. Branches and thorns lash at her arms and legs, leaving scrapes and bruises. She frequently trips, colliding with trees and snagging on bushes, her breaths labored and
her voice reduced to a faint whimper.

In the distance, the LIGHTS of a vehicle appear on a road cutting through the forest.
With the last of her strength, LUCY stumbles toward the road, moaning with pain
and fear.

LUCY (SOFT, DESPERATE)
Help… please…

EXT. COUNTRY ROAD AT THE EDGE OF THE WOODS – NIGHT

LUCY emerges, gasping for air as she reaches the ROAD. Her legs give out, and she
collapses onto the ASPHALT. A CAR approaches in the distance, HEADLIGHTS illuminating the darkness. The glare blinds her momentarily, but she musters the energy
to raise her HEAD and ARM, silently pleading for help.

The VEHICLE screeches to a halt just meters away, its HEADLIGHTS bathing LUCY in
harsh light. She shivers, covered in scratches.

A MAN (50s) and a WOMAN (50s) rush out of the CAR, hurrying toward LUCY.

WOMAN (ALARMED)

Oh God, what happened to her?

MAN (CONCERNED)

Stay still, we're here to help you. You'll be all right.

The WOMAN crouches beside LUCY, gently touching her shoulder. The MAN glances around anxiously, as if checking for danger.

WOMAN (SOFTLY, TO LUCY)

It's okay, we've got you. You're safe now.

The WOMAN jumps up, hurries to the TRUNK, and pulls out a BLANKET. She wraps it around LUCY's shoulders. LUCY tries to speak, but only a faint whisper emerges.

MAN (FIRMLY)

I'm calling the police and an ambulance.
Stay with her.

He pulls out his PHONE, walking a short distance away to make the call. Meanwhile, the WOMAN holds LUCY, speaking to her in reassuring tones. LUCY sits on the cold pavement, sobbing softly, relieved that she's no longer alone.

INT./EXT. STEVE'S CAR – EVENING

STEVE (42) is driving his FORD RANGER through the city at night, heading toward the HOTEL where ALICE (38) is staying. The glow of streetlights drifts across the windshield. It's been a long day, and the tension is palpable.

ALICE (THOUGHTFUL)

I still can't believe what Doris told us. And the
professor… something just doesn't add up.

STEVE nods, eyes on the road.

STEVE (QUIETLY, AGREEING)

Yeah, the clinic is the key. I'm sure of it. But try getting anyone else to believe that. The mayor, my colleagues—they think it's all just rumors and ghost stories. We won't get support from them.

ALICE (HALF TO HERSELF) At least
we have a bit more clarity now. But it still feels like it's
not enough. These conspiracies, the weird happe-
nings… I'm afraid no one will take it seriously.

STEVE exhales, taking a turn.

                    STEVE (PENSIVELY)

          We need more evidence, or someone who'll back us
          up. Otherwise, we're on our own here.

Suddenly, STEVE's PHONE rings. He glances at ALICE, then answers and switches to speaker.

                    COLLEAGUE (V.O.)

          Hey Steve, it's Fischer. Listen, we just picked up a
          woman who's been telling some crazy stuff about the
          old clinic. She's in pretty bad shape and they're ta-
          king her by ambulance to the hospital. Thought you
          might want to know, in case it ties into your case.

                    STEVE (ALERT)

          Got it, thanks! Any idea who she is?

                    COLLEAGUE (V.O.)

          No name yet. She keeps talking about something
          dark at the clinic. That's all I know. The ambulance is
          taking her to St. Mary's right now.

                    STEVE

          Understood, thanks. I'll look into it.

He hangs up, meeting ALICE's expectant gaze.

                    ALICE (CONCERNED)

          A woman? Who could it be? This might be our
          chance to learn more!

                    STEVE (DETERMINED)

           Then forget the hotel—let's go straight to St. Mary's. Maybe
          we'll finally get some answers there.

He flicks the TURN SIGNAL on, making a quick turn as the CAR speeds up. ALICE exhales audibly, a mix of relief and renewed tension. The streetlights pass by in a blur as
they drive into the darkness, following this new lead.

EXT. FOREST ROAD – NIGHT

An AMBULANCE is parked with its REAR DOORS open on a dark country road winding through the woods. FLASHING LIGHTS and SIRENS pierce the silence. LUCY (19) is gently lifted onto a STRETCHER by PARAMEDICS and loaded into the ambulance. A POLICE OFFICER (40s) stands beside the vehicle, glancing at his NOTES and conferring with two COLLEAGUES.

> OFFICER (CALM, PERPLEXED)
> Couldn't get much out of her. She kept calling for someone named Paul and said something terrible   happened at the old clinic. Whether this is a violent crime, I can't   say yet.

PARAMEDICS shut the AMBULANCE doors, climb inside, and speed off, SIREN wailing and LIGHTS flashing. Left behind are a few POLICE OFFICERS and the MIDDLE-AGED COUPLE (50s) who found Lucy. The couple stands a short distance away, visibly shaken.

Another OFFICER (30s), who was just taking the couple's statement, joins the small group of colleagues.

OFFICER 2 (SHAKING HIS HEAD)

They didn't have much to add. They just saw the girl collapse onto the road. They were really upset. I took down their info and sent them home.

Behind him, the couple's CAR pulls away, its TAILLIGHTS disappearing into the night. Now only two POLICE CRUISERS remain on the otherwise empty road.

> OFFICER (THINKING)
> Okay. One car heads back to the station, report what happened. The other will take a quick look at the clinic— just to make sure there's no immediate issue.

> OFFICER 2 (NODDING)
> And tomorrow morning we go in with more manpower, if there's anything to investigate at all.

The OFFICERS exchange nods and split up, getting into the two PATROL CARS. Engines rev, HEADLIGHTS sweep across the trees, and the vehicles drive off. The road falls dark again, no sign of the recent commotion remaining.

INT. HOSPITAL ROOM – NIGHT

LUCY (19) lies in a hospital bed, covered in bandages and dressings. She is asleep, clearly exhausted. Beside the bed stand an IV pole and monitors that beep at regular intervals. ALICE (38) and STEVE (42) stand by the door with a DOCTOR (50s), who is providing an update.

DOCTOR (QUIET, FACTUAL)

Physically, she's fine—mostly scrapes and bruises. But the psychological stress was high. We had to give her a sedative so she could rest.

STEVE glances anxiously at LUCY, who is sleeping soundly.

STEVE (SOFTLY)

So we can't question her yet?

The DOCTOR nods briefly.

DOCTOR

Not before tomorrow morning. She needs the rest.

He walks out into the CORRIDOR with ALICE and STEVE. Partway down the hallway, the DOCTOR stops.

DOCTOR (MEANINGFULLY) (CONT'D)

I'm sorry, I have other patients to attend to. But feel free to wait, or come back in the morning.

He leaves them and heads off to another ward. ALICE and STEVE exchange a short, uncertain glance.

Just then, one of STEVE's COLLEAGUES (30s) approaches.

COLLEAGUE (QUIETLY)

Hey Steve. Still nothing from the old clinic. Our guys are there, but no clear leads yet. I'll keep you posted.

STEVE nods, looking tense. The COLLEAGUE moves on. Now the remaining DOC-
TORS and NURSES emerge from LUCY's room, quietly discussing her condition as
they leave. LUCY remains alone in the bed, fast asleep.

ALICE and STEVE step once more to the door, casting a final look at the sleeping
LUCY. A NURSE (40s) closes the DOOR from inside, leaving only the muted glow of the
hospital corridor.

INT. ABANDONED PSYCHIATRIC CLINIC – NIGHT

Two POLICE OFFICERS (30s, 40s) enter the dim corridors of the derelict clinic, FLASH-
LIGHTS in hand. Paint flakes off the walls, debris is scattered everywhere, and the air is
thick with mold and dust.

OFFICER 1 (QUIETLY, FRUSTRATED)

This is like searching for a needle in a haystack. We're not
gonna find anything in here.

OFFICER 2 (HUSHED TONE)

Still, we got word something might've happened here. We
might stumble on evidence of those backpackers.

Their FLASHLIGHTS glide over decaying furniture and ragged beds. RATS scuttle
through the beams of light, causing them to jump momentarily. Somewhere in the distance, water drips, echoing ominously.

OFFICER 1 (CALLING OUT)

Paul! … Paul!   Anyone here?

No response, just the faint scratching and squeaking of rats. The officers exchange weary
looks, resignation clear on their faces.

OFFICER 2 (CLENCHING TEETH)

This is insane. We can barely see anything at night.

OFFICER 1 nods, shining his FLASHLIGHT across the damaged CEILING.

OFFICER 1 (DECISIVELY)

Let's call it off. This isn't getting us anywhere. Wandering

around here in the middle of the night is pointless. We'll
come back tomorrow in daylight.

They turn around and retrace their steps toward the exit. A slight rustle in the distance
makes them pause, but it's just another rodent darting among the rubble.

OFFICER 2 (RELIEVED YET TENSE)

Yeah, let's get out of here. I've had enough.

They leave the corridor, disappearing into the darkness toward the ENTRANCE,
making their way back outside – the night's search in the clinic ended in vain.

EXT. HOTEL – NIGHT

STEVE (42) pulls up in his FORD RANGER in front of the HOTEL entrance. ALICE
(38) is in the passenger seat. The night is quiet, with only a few passersby nearby.

ALICE (SOFTLY, TIRED)

So we'll meet again tomorrow morning and head straight to the hospital, right?

STEVE (NODDING) Exactly.

I'll text you about the time.

Suddenly, **STEVE'**s PHONE rings. He glances apologetically at ALICE before answering.

STEVE (INTO PHONE) (CONT'D)

Hey… Amanda…

AMANDA (V.O.) (AUDIBLY IRRITATED)

Are you coming by tonight or what?

STEVE shifts awkwardly, trying to keep ALICE from overhearing too much, but the cab
of the car is cramped.

                    STEVE (QUIET, EMBARRASSED)

      Uh, that's not happening tonight.

      I… need to swing by the station again because
      of what happened. I'll call you after, okay?

A frustrated huff from the other end.

                    AMANDA (V.O.) (ANGRY)

      You know what? Enough with the excuses. Pick up your
      stuff sometime—I'm done with this kind of relationship!

A click, and the call ends. STEVE pockets his phone, clearly unsettled, aware that
ALICE overheard at least part of it.

                    STEVE (SOFTLY, APOLOGETIC)
      Sorry… that was… nothing important. Have a good
      night, Alice.

                    ALICE (WITH GENTLE UNDERSTANDING)

      It's all right… Thanks for everything today. Sleep well.

STEVE offers a brief, uneasy smile as ALICE opens the passenger door and
steps out. She closes it gently.

She turns back for one last glance, giving STEVE a quick wave as he drives off. Then
she heads through the HOTEL DOOR and disappears inside.

INT. POLICE STATION – NIGHT

STEVE (42) enters the station, visibly exhausted. His colleague FISCHER (30s) is at
a desk in the reception area, surrounded by files and computers.

                    FISCHER (INFORMATIVE)

      Hey Steve, the guys are back from the clinic. Didn't find
      anything to back up Lucy's story. They called off the search
      and plan to go back tomorrow morning.

STEVE (ANNOYED)

Nothing at all? She was terrified—there must be something out there.

Suddenly, the CHIEF, HANK OBAMA (62), appears, looking displeased. Several other OFFICERS (30s, 40s) who also returned from the clinic stand nearby.

HANK OBAMA (GRUFF)

So? Still no results. Another case I have to explain
to the mayor. I'm running out of ways to sugarcoat
this.

The OFFICERS who were at the clinic look uneasy. HANK beckons them closer.

HANK OBAMA (STERNLY) (CONT'D)

You're going back first thing in the morning. Tear
that place apart if you have to, but don't come back
empty-handed.

One of the OFFICERS glances at STEVE uncertainly before HANK turns to STEVE.

HANK OBAMA (IRRITATED) (CONT'D)

And you, Miles—what were you thinking, bringing
that Alice woman to the hospital with you? She's stir-
red up nothing but trouble. Look at this mess—it's all
blown up for no reason.

STEVE (ATTEMPTING TO DEFEND HIMSELF)
Chief, I was just– The professor

said things, and so did Doris. Something's definitely off with that clinic. We need–

HANK OBAMA (CUTTING HIM OFF)

I don't want to hear it! You're done for the night. Meeting
adjourned!

He waves dismissively, dismissing the group. The OFFICERS head out, and HANK
disappears into his office. STEVE stands there, angry and embarrassed. He takes out
his PHONE, dialing AMANDA.

STEVE (INTO PHONE)
Amanda? Look, I'm sorry about–

The call abruptly ends. STEVE checks the screen, realizing AMANDA has hung up on him.

STEVE (QUIETLY, FRUSTRATED)(CONT'D)

Great…

He pockets his PHONE, mutters a curse under his breath, and storms out of the station, clearly annoyed.

INT. INCA TEMPLE (DREAM) – TIME UNKNOWN

TORCHES cast flickering light on stone WALLS, covered in Inca symbols and eerie carvings. ALICE (38) walks down a CORRIDOR with growing unease. OMINOUS STATUES with empty, lifeless EYES seem to watch her every move.

Suddenly, the CORRIDOR opens into a vast HALL, dominated by a colossal DAIS at the far end. Seated on a THRONE is SUPAY, the God of the Dead. Though his appearance is youthful (around 30), his shining INCA ROBES and imposing aura make it clear he is no ordinary being.

SUPAY mutters in a language unknown to modern ears, locking his gaze on ALICE with a malevolent grin, beckoning her closer.

ALICE (FEARFUL, UNDER HER BREATH)

Who… who are you? What do you want from me?

SUPAY (IN ANCIENT INCA LANGUAGE, UNINTELLIGIBLE)

Ominous, whispered incantations

ALICE hesitates, heart pounding. Yet she feels an irresistible pull.

ALICE (LOUDER, UNCERTAIN)

I don't understand! Please, if you can hear me…

(voice trembling)

…do you have my son? Where is Dennis?

SUPAY continues speaking in his strange tongue, voice more insistent now. He raises his right HAND, pointing at ALICE. His EYES gleam with an ancient, hidden power.

SUPAY (DARK WHISPER, INCA LANGUAGE)

Menacing phrases, reverberating through the hall

ALICE (PLEADING)

What… what are you saying? I… I don't understand!

SUPAY smirks cruelly. Then he speaks more forcefully, still in the old Inca language, his words echoing as if a timeless curse.

SUPAY (ANCIENT INCA, COMMANDING)
Deep, foreboding utterances

ALICE (DESPERATE)

Give me back my son! I beg you!

For a moment, SUPAY grows still, the smirk fading from his face. ALICE thinks she sees a flicker of empathy in his

gaze—until his expression suddenly darkens. He rises smoothly from the THRONE, levitating like a SPECTER.

SUPAY (DEEP, THREATENING VOICE)

One fierce, unearthly word

With a demonic SCREAM, he hurtles toward ALICE. As he soars, his once divine features warp into the visage of a decaying, zombie-like CREATURE. His splendid robes shred into bloody tatters.

ALICE (HORRIFIED, SHOUTING)

NO! PLEASE!

She stumbles backward, but SUPAY reaches her in an instant, clasping her ARM in his skeletal, rotting HANDS.

INT. HOTEL ROOM – NIGHT

In that moment, ALICE jolts awake in her BED, drenched in sweat, eyes wide with terror. It takes her several seconds to realize she's back in reality. Completely shaken, she gasps for breath and then breaks down in sobs.

INT. HOSPITAL CORRIDOR – DAY

STEVE (42) stands with his CHIEF, HANK OBAMA (62), outside the closed DOOR to LUCY (19)'s hospital room. The hallway bustles softly with typical hospital activity—footsteps and low murmurs.

                    HANK OBAMA (STERN)

        Listen, Miles. We're doing this without any supernatural
        nonsense. Keep your questions focused. I don't want to
        hear any talk about demons or what have you.

                    STEVE (CALM BUT FIRM)

        Chief, with all due respect, the woman is clearly trauma-
        tized and has mentioned something about the clinic that—

                    HANK OBAMA (CUTTING HIM OFF)

        I don't care! I want no ghost stories. We need something
        concrete, got it?

At that moment, ALICE (38) comes around the corner. She looks exhausted but offers a polite greeting when she sees STEVE and HANK.

                    ALICE

        Good morning, Steve… Chief Obama.

HANK's expression darkens noticeably, betraying his annoyance.

                    HANK OBAMA (BLUNT)

          Ah, Ms. Walker…

He clears his throat, then addresses STEVE.

                HANK OBAMA (FIRMLY)(CONT'D)

          You're coming in there with me. We're conducting
          the interview now.

                    (points to the door)

          And as for you, Ms. Walker, you don't belong here.
          Go on, get out.

                    ALICE (SHOCKED, INDIGNANT)

          What? But...

HANK raises a hand to silence her.

                    HANK OBAMA (CURT)

          I said leave. Now.

ALICE stands there, stunned, anger and disappointment warring in her eyes.

                    STEVE (QUIETLY, APOLOGETIC)

          I´m sorry, Alice...

He shrugs helplessly and follows HANK into the room. As the DOOR closes, ALICE remains in the CORRIDOR, torn between frustration and helplessness, while the interrogation proceeds behind the closed door.

INT. ABANDONED PSYCHIATRIC CLINIC – CORRIDOR – MORNING

The first rays of sunlight filter through the dusty WINDOWS, casting pale light across the decayed CORRIDOR. A POLICEMAN walks slowly down the hallway, his FOOTSTEPS echoing as he peers into the ROOMS. Occasionally, he pulls out his FLASHLIGHT, switches it on, and scans shadowy corners before moving on.

His RADIO crackles, followed by the voice of a colleague.

COLLEAGUE (OVER RADIO)

I think I found something. Can you come up here?

The POLICEMAN grabs his RADIO.

POLICEMAN

On my way.

He clips the RADIO and FLASHLIGHT back onto his belt, turns, and heads toward the nearest STAIRCASE.

INT. ABANDONED PSYCHIATRIC CLINIC – UPPER FLOOR – MORNING

Another POLICEMAN crouches on the floor of a ROOM. Around him are scattered personal ITEMS: backpacks, clothing, and other belongings. Using a PENCIL, he sifts through the objects.

The first POLICEMAN enters the ROOM.

FIRST POLICEMAN
What've you got?

The second POLICEMAN glances up with a slight SMIRK.

SECOND POLICEMAN

Looks like the girl's stuff… and her so-called boyfriend's.

He lifts a BRA with his PENCIL, grinning.

SECOND POLICEMAN (SARCASTIC) (CONT'D)

Evidence is piling up, huh?

Both chuckle quietly. They continue searching through the belongings. The first POLICEMAN finds a small bag of JOINTS, while the second holds up a tube of PILLS.

FIRST POLICEMAN

Well, that explains a lot.

SECOND POLICEMAN

Too many drugs, probably. The girl lost it, and her
boyfriend bailed.

FIRST POLICEMAN

He'll turn up somewhere, hungover and clueless.

The two POLICEMEN decide to pack up the BACKPACKERS' belongings. They
gather everything and stow it in a BAG.

FIRST POLICEMAN (CONT'D)

That's enough for now. Let's head back.

They leave the ROOM, their FOOTSTEPS echoing in the quiet CLINIC as the last
beams of morning sunlight filter through the windows.

INT. HOSPITAL ROOM – MORNING

STEVE (42) and his CHIEF, HANK OBAMA (62), stand by the hospital BED of LUCY
(19). Lucy looks exhausted and distraught, her eyes red and her voice shaky. STEVE
holds a NOTEPAD and PEN, ready to take notes.

STEVE (GENTLY)

Lucy, I know this is very hard for you. But we need to
understand what happened. Can you tell us?

LUCY hesitates, searching for the words before she begins.

LUCY (TREMBLING)

It started with the noises. They were everywhere…
scratching, whispering… and then the shadows.
They… they moved on the walls, like they were alive.

STEVE jots down her statements in bullet points.

STEVE (ENCOURAGING)

And what happened next?

LUCY (TEARFULLY)

Paul… he was suddenly dragged away. By something invisible. It… it pulled him into the dark. He
screamed, but I couldn't do anything. I just ran…

STEVE (CALMLY, REASSURING)
That's good, Lucy. And after that?

Before LUCY can respond, HANK OBAMA's phone rings. He steps back, answering
the CALL.

HANK OBAMA (INTO PHONE)
Obama here.

The voice of the POLICEMAN from the clinic comes through the line.

POLICEMAN (OVER PHONE)

Chief, there's no sign of the boyfriend.
But we did find a lot of drugs—joints, pills, the works.

HANK OBAMA (CURT)

Got it. Thanks for the update.

HANK ends the call, pockets his phone, and steps back to the BED. He looks at LUCY
with a stern expression.

HANK OBAMA (COOLLY) (CONT'D)

Lucy, we've discovered there were a lot of drugs involved. Was this a party that got out of hand?

LUCY (DESPERATE, CRYING)

No! It wasn't a party! You have to believe me! It was… something else…

HANK raises a dismissive hand.

HANK OBAMA (DISMISSIVE)

That's enough. We're done here.

STEVE (CUTTING IN, CONFUSED)

Chief, maybe we should—

HANK OBAMA (FIRMLY)

No, Miles. This is over.

LUCY becomes increasingly panicked, starting to sob uncontrollably. A NURSE enters the ROOM and immediately goes to LUCY. She glares at STEVE and HANK.

NURSE (SNAPPING)

That's enough! Both of you, out. Now!

HANK shrugs and heads for the door. STEVE casts a final glance at LUCY, still sobbing under the NURSE's care, before reluctantly following. The DOOR closes behind them.

INT. HOSPITAL HALLWAY – DAY

The door to LUCY's ROOM opens, and STEVE (42) and HANK OBAMA (62) step out. A few meters away, ALICE (38) sits on a chair, watching them expectantly. HANK strides past her, throwing her a brief, confused, and disdainful glance. He pulls out his PHONE and dials a number.

HANK OBAMA (TO STEVE, OVER HIS
SHOULDER)

I want you back at the station in thirty minutes. We've
got real work to do.

STEVE nods curtly. HANK pauses, glances back briefly, then continues walking down the hall, talking on his phone.

ALICE stands and takes a step toward STEVE.

ALICE (QUESTIONING)

That was fast. What happened?

STEVE stops, sighs, and shakes his head.

                    STEVE (SLIGHTLY ANNOYED)

    The drugs they found made everything worse. It's set us
    back a lot.

                    ALICE (ACCUSINGLY)

    Didn't you tell him about what the professor and Doris said?

                    STEVE (IRRITATED)

    Of course I did! I'm not an idiot, Alice. But the chief
    doesn't want to hear it. That's just how things are in
    this damn town.

ALICE studies STEVE, her brow furrowed. She shakes her head, her mind racing.

                    ALICE (FIRMLY)

    I'm not accepting this.

STEVE glances at his watch, realizing he's running out of time.

                    STEVE (APOLOGETICALLY)

    Alice, I get it. I really do. But I have to go. I'm sorry.
    Please understand.

ALICE crosses her arms, visibly upset and angry.

                    ALICE (SHARPLY)

    Fine, Steve. Go. But you'll see.

STEVE gives her a questioning look but says nothing. Instead, he turns and walks
quickly down the HALLWAY. ALICE remains behind, her frustration and determination
etched on her face.

INT. MAYOR DONALD ABRAHAM'S KITCHEN – MORNING

The MAYOR, DONALD ABRAHAM (53), stands in his large, modern KITCHEN. With
one hand, he tries to put on a SHIRT while holding his PHONE in the other, talking to
HANK OBAMA (62). His expression is one of irritation.

MAYOR DONALD ABRAHAM (INTO PHONE, ANNOYED)

Hank, I told you I don't want to hear about these missing persons anymore. There are more important things than these fairy tales!

He struggles to button his SHIRT one-handed. His WIFE, LILLIAN ABRAHAM (49), places a CUP OF COFFEE on the counter with a nod. He barely acknowledges her.

HANK OBAMA (FROM PHONE)
We've got a new case, but it looks like it's just drug-related. Shouldn't be a big deal.

The Mayor exhales in relief, his mood slightly improving.

MAYOR DONALD ABRAHAM (INTO PHONE)
There you go, Hank! These things

sort themselves out. Just don't bother me with it again, got it?

Without waiting for a reply, he hangs up and pockets the PHONE. He takes a SIP of COFFEE and winces as he burns his mouth.

MAYOR DONALD ABRAHAM (ANNOYED) (CONT'D)

Lillien, the coffee is hot! A little warning would be nice!

LILLIAN ABRAHAM rolls her eyes and leaves the KITCHEN without a word. The Mayor focuses on buttoning his SHIRT, managing better this time.

Just then, his DAUGHTER, AMELIA ABRAHAM (17), storms into the kitchen. She plants herself in front of him, arms crossed.

AMELIA ABRAHAM (ACCUSING)

Do you even know what day it is the day after tomorrow?

DONALD frowns as he rolls up his sleeves.

MAYOR DONALD ABRAHAM (CLUELESS)
No, what's happening the day after tomorrow?

AMELIA ABRAHAM's face flushes with anger.

AMELIA ABRAHAM (YELLING)

My birthday, Dad! But you don't care, do you?

With tears welling up, she spins around and storms out of the KITCHEN. The Mayor stands there, dumbfounded, completely thrown by her outburst.

MAYOR DONALD ABRAHAM (MUTTERING)
Everyone's losing their minds

around here…

He grabs his JACKET from a chair, puts it on, and leaves the KITCHEN as well.

INT. CAFE – MORNING

A cozy, somewhat busy CAFE. ALICE (38) and JACOB WALSH (48), a reporter, sit across from each other at a small TABLE. On the TABLE lie JACOB's NOTEPAD and PEN, alongside ALICE's cup of COFFEE, from which she takes occasional sips.

JACOB (WRITING NOTES)

So, we have the old rumors about the clinic, the disappearance of your son Dennis and his friend Tom, and now
this Paul as well. And from what you're saying, nobody in
town seems willing to do much about it.

ALICE (RESIGNED)

Exactly. That's the issue. I feel like everyone's just looking
the other way. And now that they found drugs in the clinic,
it's even more complicated.

JACOB (LOOKS UP, EMPATHETIC)

I understand your frustration, Alice. I'll try to write an
article about it. Can't promise anything—my editor has the
final say.

(offers a faint encouraging
smile)

But he isn't the mayor's biggest fan, so there's a decent
chance.

ALICE (RELIEVED, TAKING A SIP OF
COFFEE)

Thank you. It's good to know someone's finally
listening and ready to make it public. Maybe
that'll wake people up.

JACOB closes his NOTEPAD, slipping it into his jacket pocket.

JACOB

I'll get in touch if I have more questions. Thanks
for trusting me with this.

ALICE (GRATEFUL)

Thank you, Jacob. I'm really counting on you.

JACOB stands, bids her a brief farewell with a nod, and exits the CAFE. ALICE watches
him go, then picks up her PHONE and dials.

STEVE (O.S.) (OVER THE PHONE)

Hey, Alice. What's up?

ALICE (QUIET, RESOLUTE)

I just spoke with a reporter, Jacob Walsh. He might publish
an article on everything tomorrow.

A brief pause on the other end.

STEVE (O.S.) (CALM, WORRIED)

An article... you know what that's gonna stir up.

ALICE (WITH SLIGHT SARCASM)

I don't care. Somebody has to act. Everyone's been ignoring this for too long.

STEVE (O.S.) (SIGHING)

All right. When do we meet?

ALICE (THINKING)

Tonight at the bar, near the hotel. Around eight?

STEVE (O.S.) (HESITANT)

Okay, eight o'clock at the bar. We'll see what we
can do from there.

ALICE (FIRM)

Thanks, Steve. We need every step we can take.

STEVE (O.S.)

Got it. Talk to you then.

ALICE ends the call. Setting the PHONE aside, she takes another sip of COFFEE, her face reflecting both relief and lingering tension. The muffled sounds of other patrons and clinking dishes fill the background as the scene fades out.

INT. POLICE STATION – BRIEFING ROOM – MORNING

Several POLICE OFFICERS, including STEVE (42) and his COLLEAGUES, sit around a large TABLE. The ROOM is functional, with DUTY ROSTERS and a WHITEBOARD on the walls. At the front stands the CHIEF, HANK OBAMA (62), having a brief exchange with the MAYOR, DONALD ABRAHAM (53).

STEVE pockets his PHONE and takes a seat among his peers. The MAYOR casts STEVE a sullen glance as he exits. Once he's gone, HANK lifts his head to commence the daily BRIEFING.

HANK OBAMA (CALMLY, FIRMLY)

All right, folks. First item: that so-called missing backpacker. We've got indications it's just a drug situation. No
need to keep searching—he'll show up sooner or later.
Then we'll deal with it.

STEVE clenches his jaw, frowning. Some of his COLLEAGUES exchange glances but remain silent. HANK is about to move on.

STEVE (RESOLUTE)

Chief, I have to disagree. We have facts pointing to

more than just drugs. Alice Walker and I—

                    HANK OBAMA (CUTS HIM OFF SHARPLY)

Miles! Did you not hear what I said? We don't have time to
chase after every rumor. The MAYOR's sick of it, too.

                    STEVE (HEATED, STANDS)

But these aren't rumors! The professor, Doris Evens—
there's evidence something's really off here. We can't just—

                    HANK OBAMA (RAISING HIS VOICE, ANGRY)
Enough! If you can't learn to

follow orders, you're free to leave.

                    (gestures forcefully toward th door)

Understood?

An awkward hush falls. STEVE looks around, but his COLLEAGUES avoid meeting his
gaze; none want to get involved. Eventually, STEVE sighs and sits back down.

                    STEVE (DEFEATED)
        …Yes, Chief.

HANK takes a moment to regain composure, visibly irritated, then proceeds.

                    HANK OBAMA (DELIBERATELY)
Good. Next item: The traffic light failure on Main
Street. We need a team on that immediately.

The CAMERA lingers on STEVE, who stares ahead in silence while HANK OBAMA
continues detailing the next AGENDA POINT.

INT. AMELIA ABRAHAM'S ROOM – DAY

AMELIA ABRAHAM (17) lies on her BED, distractedly scrolling on her PHONE, looking glum. Standing in front of the bed is TRACY (17), her best friend, attempting to
cheer her up.

                    TRACY (COMFORTING)

Hey, don't worry. If your dad won't throw you a party,

we'll just do it ourselves—and it'll be one you'll never
forget. You only turn eighteen once!

AMELIA ABRAHAM glances up, her expression brightening a bit.

                    AMELIA ABRAHAM (CURIOUS)

        Seriously? So how's it gonna work? Where, who's co-
        ming… I need details!

TRACY laughs, raising her hands in a playful gesture.

                    TRACY (LAUGHING)

        You'll just have to wait and see! It's my gift to you. Trust
        me, it'll be epic.

AMELIA ABRAHAM sits up, putting her PHONE aside. Her eyes shine with sudden
excitement.

                    AMELIA ABRAHAM (EXCITED)

        Oh my God, Tracy, you're the best! I can't wait!

TRACY grins, grabs AMELIA ABRAHAM's hands, and the two of them start jum-
ping on the BED like little kids, squealing with delight.

                    AMELIA ABRAHAM (LAUGHING)(CONT'D)

        This is gonna be awesome!

Their carefree laughter fills the room as they momentarily forget their worries, bouncing up and down on the bed.

INT. BAR – EVENING

The BAR is dimly lit, filled with soft background music and the low murmur of patrons.
STEVE (42) enters, goes straight to the BARTENDER, and orders a BEER. Then he
spots ALICE (38) seated at a WINDOW TABLE, multiple NOTES spread out before her
like a battle plan, with a half-full glass of WINE on one of the papers.

                    STEVE (CAUTIOUSLY SMILING)

        Hey, Alice.

ALICE (LOOKS UP, RETURNS A SMALL SMILE)

Steve! Glad you could make it.

STEVE takes his BEER, weaves through the patrons, and sits across from ALICE, eyeing the spread of PAPERS with slight disbelief.

STEVE (CURIOUS)

Wow… you've really gone all in. What's all this?

ALICE (ENTHUSIASTIC)

These are my notes, my research. Every clue we've got so far, I put them all together. See here?

(pointing to a paper)

This is Doris's tip, and this one is about the professor… Everything points to that clinic. I'm sure Dennis, Tom, and now Paul vanished because of whatever's going on there. The only one not telling us everything is definitely the professor.

STEVE takes a sip of his BEER, sets the bottle down, appearing uncertain.

STEVE (QUIETLY)

Alice, I see how hard you're working. But after all the pushback at the station, and this drug mess at the clinic… I don't know. Maybe Paul will turn up. Maybe it was a huge misunderstanding.

ALICE (IN DISBELIEF)

What? What about Doris's stories, the professor's contradictions? All those missing people, you just ignore that?

STEVE (SHRUGS)

Work's been insane… My chief wants none of it. And that reporter story—once it hits tomorrow, nobody's gonna back us. The mayor'll flip, the chief too. We might be on our own. Maybe it's best to wait it out.

ALICE (ANGRY AND UPSET)

Wait it out? You're letting them get to you, Steve! I expected more from you. You know how serious this is!

STEVE (SOFTLY, BUT FIRMLY)

I get it. But I can't share your enthusiasm right now. I'm
sorry, Alice.

An awkward silence falls. ALICE glares at her NOTES, STEVE looks troubled.

STEVE (RISING)(CONT'D)

I think I'd better go. This is… sorry.

ALICE (FURIOUS)

Fine, go! But I'm going to see the professor first
thing tomorrow— with or without you!

STEVE gives a slight nod, picks up his BEER, and walks away from the TABLE. ALICE
watches him go, stunned. Then she angrily gathers her NOTES, stuffs them into her
BAG, tosses some CASH on the table to pay, and leaves the BAR in a huff.

INT. HOTEL ROOM – NIGHT

ALICE (38), just back from the BAR, sits on her BED with numerous NOTES scattered around her, reorganizing and reordering them. Her expression reveals both determination and inner turmoil.

She gives her PHONE a brief, disappointed glance, recalling STEVE's reaction at the
bar. Then she inhales deeply, as if encouraging herself.

ALICE (QUIETLY, TO HERSELF)

I've come this far… I feel like I'm on the brink of something.

(pauses, voice tense)

But I'm so afraid I'll never see Dennis again.

Resolute, she picks up the TELEPHONE and dials a number.

ALICE holds the PHONE to her ear, her tone subdued.

ALICE (ON PHONE)(CONT'D)

Hi, it's Alice. Yes... just wanted to keep you updated.

ALICE (ON PHONE) (CONT'D)

(pause)

I'm afraid the authorities aren't being very coopera-
tive, but I'm not giving up.

(short silence)

No, I'm not telling them everything yet. Anyway, I'll
call you as soon as there's any news. Thanks. Good
night.

She hangs up, placing the PHONE gently beside her. For a moment, she simply sits there, her NOTES in her lap. Her eyes threaten to well with tears, but she blinks them a-way.

Then she lies back on the BED, arms extended, gazing up at the CEILING. After a beat, she exhales sharply and closes her EYES. A faint glow from the window highlights her face as the scene slowly fades out.

INT. HOTEL ROOM – MORNING

ALICE (38) gathers the last of her NOTES and tucks them into a small SHOULDER BAG. Determination is written on her

face—she's ready to confront the PROFESSOR today. Just as she heads to the DOOR, there's a KNOCK. She stops, eyebrows furrowed.

ALICE Yes?

She opens the DOOR to find STEVE (42) standing there with a broad smile and two steaming CUPS OF COFFEE in his hands.

STEVE (APOLOGETIC, SOFTLY SMILING)

Morning... I thought I'd drop by and—well, this is for you. (offers
her one of the cups)

And... I'm sorry about last night. Really. I let the pressure get to me. But I'm fully behind you, no matter what everyone else does.

ALICE takes a moment, clearly moved and relieved.

                    ALICE (GENTLY)

        Steve… I was so worried you'd given up. I'm so glad
        you're here now.

                    STEVE (SHEEPISH GRIN)

         Couldn't let you face the professor alone. We're in this to-
        gether… and I know how much it means to you.

                    ALICE (SUDDENLY OVERCOME WITH RELIEF)

        Oh, Steve—

She throws her arms around him spontaneously. The COFFEE cups wobble, and
STEVE raises his arms quickly to keep them from spilling. Both laugh, thankful for this
reconciliation.

                    STEVE (LAUGHING)
        Easy, the coffee!

ALICE pulls away carefully, giggling. She takes one of the CUPS for herself.

                    ALICE (SMILING)

        Thank you… for everything. Really.

STEVE nods, then gestures to her BAG of NOTES.

                    STEVE
        Ready?

                    ALICE (FIRMLY)

        More than ever. Let´s go see the professor.

They step out of the ROOM, letting the DOOR click shut behind them. They share a relieved, happy look as they head

off—armed with COFFEE, a plan, and renewed resolve.

94

INT. MAYOR DONALD ABRAHAM'S KITCHEN – MORNING

Sunlight streams through the kitchen window, casting a warm glow. On the TABLE sits a small CAKE with 18 lit CANDLES. AMELIA ABRAHAM (18) enters and stops in surprise, seeing her PARENTS, DONALD ABRAHAM (53) and LILLIAN ABRAHAM ABRAHAM (49), smiling at her.

DONALD and LILLIAN ABRAHAM (loudly, in unison)

Happy Birthday, AMELIA ABRAHAM!

AMELIA ABRAHAM's eyes widen, her face lighting up with a broad smile.

AMELIA ABRAHAM (TOUCHED)

Oh wow… you actually remembered! Thank you so much.

LILLIAN ABRAHAM steps forward, hugging AMELIA ABRAHAM warmly.

LILLIAN ABRAHAM (WARMLY)
Happy birthday, sweetheart!

DONALD also hugs his DAUGHTER.

MAYOR DONALD ABRAHAM

Happy birthday, AMELIA ABRAHAM. I'm so happy for you.

AMELIA ABRAHAM looks at the cake with its flickering CANDLES, stepping closer to the TABLE.

LILLIAN ABRAHAM (SMILING)

Blow out the candles and make a wish.

AMELIA ABRAHAM leans over, blowing out the 18 CANDLES. Smoke drifts upward, and she briefly closes her eyes.

AMELIA ABRAHAM (SOFTLY)

So… I'm finally 18.

DONALD ABRAHAM puts a hand on her shoulder and leads her aside for a private word.

>
>   MAYOR DONALD ABRAHAM (QUIET,
>   APOLOGETIC)
>
> I know you wanted a big party today. But you've
> seen how hectic it is—there's all this work with the
> tourists, the commotion in town. I had to postpone
> the celebration.

>
>   AMELIA ABRAHAM (A BIT DISAPPOINTED, BUT
>   UNDERSTANDING)
>
> It's okay, Dad. I just thought maybe you didn't
> care about my birthday at all.

>
>   MAYOR DONALD ABRAHAM (EMPHATIC) I
> do care, very much. I promise
>
> you: once the busy season slows down, we'll
> make it a huge celebration. One you'll never for-
> get.

>
>   AMELIA ABRAHAM (LAUGHING)
>
> All right. I'll let you surprise   me.

MAYOR DONALD ABRAHAM   exhales in relief, putting his arm around LILLIAN ABRA-
HAM, who stands by smiling. They watch happily as AMELIA ABRAHAM goes to the
CAKE, lightly running a finger across the extinguished candles.

>
>   LILLIAN ABRAHAM
>
> We've also got some presents for you… and you
> get to decide what we do today.

>
>   AMELIA ABRAHAM (CURIOUS)
>
> Oh? Let's see.

AMELIA ABRAHAM sits at the TABLE, opens a small BOX, and bursts out laughing with
joy at what she finds inside. DONALD and LILLIAN ABRAHAM exchange pleased looks
as their now officially 18-year-old DAUGHTER beams at her gifts.

INT. AMELIA ABRAHAM'S ROOM – LATER IN THE DAY

Warm light fills the room. AMELIA ABRAHAM (18) lies on her BED, PHONE pressed to her ear. On her bedside table is a PLATE with a slice of birthday cake and some of the GIFTS she received that morning.

                    AMELIA ABRAHAM (RELAXED, BUT EXCITED)

        Hey, Tracy, thanks for calling... yeah, birthday and all that.

We hear TRACY (O.S.) on the other end, equally enthusiastic.

                    TRACY (O.S.)

        Of course! Happy Birthday! Ready for tonight?
        I'm so excited!

AMELIA ABRAHAM laughs, rolling onto her side, her gaze drifting to a small OPEN GIFT BOX nearby.

                    AMELIA ABRAHAM (CURIOUS)

        So, spill—where's the party happening? Who's coming?
        You haven't told me anything!

                    TRACY (O.S.) (GIGGLING)

        You'll see. But let's just say the cool guys from school will
        be there, you know, the football crew...

                    AMELIA ABRAHAM (BIG GRIN)

        Seriously? That's awesome! But you know how weird my
        dad's been. Can I even get out of the house?

                    TRACY (O.S.)

        Don't worry. Just say you're staying over at my place—
        works every time. Add some puppy-dog eyes for good
        measure.

AMELIA ABRAHAM glances briefly at the DOOR, as if worried about being over-heard, then laughs conspiratorially.

                    AMELIA ABRAHAM

        Yeah, you're right. That's what I'll do. So the
        party's on!

TRACY (O.S.)

Totally! We have to celebrate your birthday right.
I'm so looking forward to it!

AMELIA ABRAHAM (SMILING)
Same. So that's settled.

TRACY (O.S.)

Exactly. I'll fill you in on the rest later. Hey, did you
see that new Insta post…

AMELIA ABRAHAM leans back, toying with a strand of hair.

AMELIA ABRAHAM (SOMEWHAT ABSENT-
MINDED)

Yeah, I saw it… oh, you know what… (laughs) …

As the conversation shifts to more casual topics, the CAMERA slowly pulls back. AME-
LIA ABRAHAM looks relaxed and happy, chatting with TRACY, her mind already on
the party to come.

EXT. PROFESSOR'S HOUSE – DAY

Morning sunlight falls on the old but well-maintained HOUSE. ALICE (38) and STEVE
(42) stand by the closed FRONT DOOR. ALICE looks determined; STEVE seems
slightly uneasy.

After a brief pause, ALICE knocks. A moment later, DANIEL LIVINGSTON (72),
the professor's son, opens the DOOR, frowning at the sight of them.

DANIEL (SURPRISED)

You again? What do you want now?

ALICE (FIRMLY)

We need to talk to your father. Right now.

DANIEL (REFUSING)

No, that's not possible. He's in no condition to re-
ceive visitors. You need to leave.

He attempts to close the DOOR, but ALICE presses against it. STEVE watches in astonishment as ALICE pushes past DANIEL with surprising force.

> DANIEL (STARTLED)(CONT'D)
>
> What… what do you think you're doing? Get
> out of here!

> ALICE (WITH RESOLVE)
>
> Not until I speak with the professor.

Daniel tries again to block ALICE, but she's already slipped past him into the HALLWAY. STEVE follows uncertainly, throwing Daniel an apologetic glance.

> STEVE (QUIETLY)
>
> Sorry, Daniel…

> DANIEL (AGHAST)
>
> You can't just barge in here!

But ALICE stands her ground, heart pounding yet unwavering.

> ALICE (INSISTENT)
>
> We need to see the professor. He still owes us
> answers.

For a moment, DANIEL is speechless, while STEVE hovers behind ALICE. Finally, DANIEL shuts the DOOR with a flustered motion and turns to face them both.

The camera focuses on ALICE in the entryway, locking eyes with DANIEL, ready to press forward—no matter what.

INT. PROFESSOR'S ROOM – DAY

PROFESSOR THEODOR LIVINGSTON (90+) sits as usual in his WHEELCHAIR by the WINDOW. A muffled commotion from the STAIRS drifts into the room. His withered hand rests on the arm of the chair, and he listens with irritation.

Suddenly, the DOOR bursts open. DANIEL (72) rushes in first, followed closely by

ALICE (38) and STEVE (42). DANIEL hurries to the PROFESSOR, trying breathlessly to explain.

DANIEL (ANXIOUS)

Father, I'm so sorry. They just forced their way in, I couldn't stop them!

The PROFESSOR straightens in his wheelchair, anger in his eyes. He raises his voice to express his indignation.

PROFESSOR (FROWNING, ANGRILY)
What is the meaning of this? How

dare you barge in here uninvited?

But before he can continue, ALICE steps forward, confronting him directly. STEVE stands somewhat behind her, casting an uncertain glance at DANIEL, who appears unsure how to respond.

ALICE (FIRM)

That's enough! We're done with your evasions. You know exactly what happened in that clinic. Dennis, Tom, Paul – they've all disappeared, and it must tie back to that place.

The PROFESSOR's face darkens, his hands gripping the armrests.

PROFESSOR (CUTTING)

I have no idea what you're talking about. Now get out of my house, immediately!

ALICE (LOUD, UNWAVERING) No, I
won't. I spoke with Doris, the former nurse. She told us about the uncanny things that went on in the clinic – and you know precisely what's behind it. No more lies! Tell the truth!

STEVE (TRYING TO MEDIATE)

Alice, maybe we should—

ALICE (ANGRILY CUTTING HIM OFF)

No, Steve! We deserve answers!

The PROFESSOR breathes heavily. DANIEL glances anxiously between them, power-less in the face of ALICE's determination. A tense silence fills the room, only the Profes-sor's ragged breathing breaks it.

At last, the PROFESSOR relents. His shoulders slump, and he suddenly seems very old and tired.

PROFESSOR (SOFTLY, DEFEATED)

I… I can't bear it anymore. These damned secrets are driving me mad.   Just like they did O'Kelly.

ALICE, STEVE, and DANIEL look on in astonishment. ALICE's fury mingles with sur-prise, STEVE frowns, and DANIEL appears shaken.

With a trembling voice, the PROFESSOR gestures to a few chairs.

PROFESSOR (GENTLY) (CONT'D)

Sit… all of you. I suppose it's time I told the truth.

They obey, taking seats. DANIEL stands close to the PROFESSOR, uncertain of what's about to unfold. ALICE and STEVE exchange a brief look—hopeful, yet anxious.

PROFESSOR (GATHERING HIMSELF, IN A

WHISPER) (CONT'D)

It began during one of my sessions with O'Kelly... back then...

The camera lingers on thc four of them In close proximity. Tension crackles in the air as the PROFESSOR begins to reveal the first words of his confession.

INT. PSYCHIATRIC CLINIC – TREATMENT ROOM – INDEFINITE TIME (FLASH-BACK)

In a dim, secluded ROOM of the old clinic, O'KELLY (about 30) sits in a CHAIR, wearing a STRAITJACKET, facing the PROFESSOR's DESK. On the desk lie FILES and a small tape recorder; a faint LAMP flickers overhead. O'KELLY appears sedated, his eyes glassy yet occasionally flickering as if he might snap out of his stupor.

The PROFESSOR, THEODOR LIVINGSTON (mid-60s at this time), flips through O'KELLY's FILE, glancing at him now and then. The faint TICKING of a clock punctuates the silence, along with O'KELLY's subdued groans.

PROFESSOR (QUIET, SEEKING INFO)

Mr. O'Kelly… please, try to focus.

I'm reading about your expedition in South America. Can you tell me more about… what happened there?

O'KELLY exhales shakily, his head dropping forward, then he briefly gains clarity, lifting his gaze with sudden intensity.

O'KELLY (IN A LUCID MOMENT, HOARSE)

We… found an abandoned

temple—thought it was our big break. An Inca temple, deep in the jungle. Then… it all went… horribly wrong.

He falters, eyes rolling, uttering incoherent mumbling. The PROFESSOR notes something, waiting patiently until O'KELLY's lucidity returns.

O'KELLY (AFTER A SPASM, CALMER) (CONT'D)

The locals… fled. Strange noises, voices… My team vanished, one by one. And… the worst part was this hidden chamber inside. A massive boulder… blocked it. We… we just blasted it away.

His voice trembles; the PROFESSOR tightens his grip on his PEN.

PROFESSOR

A boulder… you blasted it open?

O'KELLY (TREMBLING)

We shouldn't have. Behind it was a room, with an invisible barrier. In front, everything decayed, ancient. But behind… it glowed, torches reflecting off golden mirrors. It felt like… a curse.

(pauses)

None of them dared go in, except me. My curiosity was too strong.

He slumps, breathing labored. The PROFESSOR watches, growing uneasy. After several moments, O'KELLY lifts his head again.

O'KELLY (HALTING, HAUNTED) (CONT'D)

I… I went through. It was so bright, golden orna-
ments, huge statues. Then… a man in splendid robes appeared, speaking a tongue I couldn't understand. He pulled me toward him with just a gesture.

O'KELLY's eyes widen as if reliving a hidden terror, his body shaking.

O'KELLY (IN TORMENT) (CONT'D)

Supay… the God of the Dead. His hand on my
forehead…

(He groans)

All I saw were dark figures, reaching for me, and
heard Supay's demonic voice… words I couldn't
comprehend. Then… it ended. The barrier was gone,
my crew was gone. I was alone.

He suddenly seizes in another fit, the PROFESSOR recoiling slightly in uncertainty.
Once O'KELLY settles somewhat, he continues:

O'KELLY (RASPY, NEAR TEARS) (CONT'D)

Something terrible happened to me. I… fled, wande-
red the jungle for weeks. Finally… natives got me to
the coast. On the ship, people started disappearing. I
realized it was tied to me, to what happened in that
temple.

His voice gives way to gibberish as he slides back into delirium. The PROFESSOR
sighs, setting aside his NOTES. He looks at O'KELLY, whose convulsions subside
into sedated stupor. Concern and fear flicker in the PROFESSOR's expression,
unsure what to believe.

The camera lingers on the PROFESSOR as he closes the FILE and glances toward the
ROOM´S EXIT, face etched with confusion, before the scene fades out.

INT. PROFESSOR'S ROOM – DAY

ALICE (38), STEVE (42), and DANIEL LIVINGSTON (72) sit intently on CHAIRS facing the PROFESSOR (90+), who is seated in his WHEELCHAIR by the WINDOW. The tension in the air is palpable as the PROFESSOR struggles for breath, trying to continue his tale. Only the TICKING of a grandfather clock and the soft breathing of the listeners break the silence.

              PROFESSOR (EXHAUSTED BUT EMPHATIC)

        At first... I thought O'Kelly was schizophrenic. A wild imagina-
        tion. A madman we had to keep sedated. I didn't believe a word
        he said.

He pauses briefly. His hands tremble, his gaze shifting to DANIEL, who looks dismayed.

              PROFESSOR (CONTINUING)(CONT'D)

        But then... patients started disappearing, again
        and again. The clinic management said they
        simply broke out, ran away. Some of them,
        sure... but others vanished without a trace.

STEVE throws ALICE an alarmed glance, but they both remain silent, listening.

              PROFESSOR (QUIETLY, VOICE TREMBLING)(CONT'D)

        Staff members, too, began to go missing—nur-
        ses, orderlies. The press caught wind of it. We
        could no longer cover it up. I couldn't decide
        whether to believe O'Kelly's delusions or the
        rumors.

DANIEL leans forward, places a hand on his father's arm, as the PROFESSOR continues, shaking.

              DANIEL (SOFTLY, CONCERNED)
        Father... maybe that's enough.

The PROFESSOR shakes his head, his eyes now filled with resolve, as if dispelling all doubt.

              PROFESSOR (FRAIL BUT RESOLUTE)
        No, Daniel. I... I have to finish. I

        can't remain silent. (brief

pause)

O'Kelly's seizures got worse; he had full-blown screaming fits, speaking that incomprehensible language as though possessed... So we had to keep him heavily sedated, tied to his bed. But with the outside pressure... the scandal... we couldn't stop it. The clinic... lost its reputation... it escalated.

ALICE (AWED)

So... you now believe O'Kelly might have been right? That he brought something back from that Inca temple?

The PROFESSOR remains silent for a moment, then weakly nods.

PROFESSOR

The events... point to it. He spoke of a force he unwittingly unleashed.

PROFESSOR (CONT'D)

I... refused to believe it. But with every disappearance, my skepticism weakened.

His head droops, his voice rough.

PROFESSOR (CONT'D)

I couldn't keep dismissing O'Kelly as insane. But... what if he... what if he really did bring this... curse with him?

He tries to breathe, fighting for strength. DANIEL places a hand on the PROFESSOR's shoulder, but the PROFESSOR barely reacts.

STEVE (CAUTIOUSLY)

Professor... this is incredible. But what does it mean for now? What exactly happened to O'Kelly?

INT. PSYCHIATRIC CLINIC – CORRIDOR – INDEFINITE TIME (FLASH-BACK)

A dimly lit CORRIDOR in the old clinic. The PROFESSOR (mid-60s) hurries down the HALL, tension etched on his face. A NURSE or ORDERLY stands near a DOOR, loo- king panicked.

ORDERLY (BREATHING HEAVILY)

Professor, come quick… something terrible's happened!

The PROFESSOR glances at him in alarm and speeds up, pushing the DOOR open with urgency.

INT. PSYCHIATRIC CLINIC – O'KELLY'S ROOM – CONTINUOUS

As soon as the PROFESSOR enters, he stops short: O'KELLY lies on his BED, soaked in BLOOD. One ARM has freed itself from restraints and dangles limply off the edge of the mattress. In his HAND, he clutches a bloodied SHARD OF GLASS, still dripping with red. A gaping NECK WOUND bleeds profusely, and O'KELLY is choking for air.

PROFESSOR (ANGRILY, TO THE ORDERLY)

How did this happen? Get help right now!

The ORDERLY steps aside, letting the PROFESSOR pass, then dashes back into the CORRIDOR

The PROFESSOR rushes to the BED, aghast at the severity of the wound, trying to stanch the bleeding with a CLOTH. Blood, however, continues to flow freely.

PROFESSOR (DESPERATE, SOOTHING

O'KELLY) (CONT'D)

Stay with me… we'll fix this… please, just
hold on.

O'KELLY's eyes are wide and frantic, staring at the CEILING. The PROFESSOR can see the wound is fatal and looks around in vain for assistance.

Suddenly, O'KELLY grabs the PROFESSOR's ARM. His gaze shifts into unexpected calm, relief washing over his face.

O'KELLY (BARELY AUDIBLE)

...let me... go...

Abruptly, BLACK VEINS spread across O'KELLY's FACE, and his EYES darken to solid black. The PROFESSOR gasps, trying to pull away, but O'KELLY holds him with surprising strength. With a grim SMILE, O'KELLY mutters in a demonic, incomprehensible TONGUE.

PROFESSOR (HORRIFIED)
O'Kelly...?

Then O'KELLY collapses, the BLACK EYES fading, his ARM going limp. He takes one final, rattling breath and dies. The PROFESSOR is left trembling, the shard of glass clattering to the floor.

At that moment, the ORDERLY and a NURSE come rushing in. They see the pool of BLOOD and the lifeless O'KELLY. The NURSE crosses herself, while the ORDERLY looks at the PROFESSOR with questions in his eyes.

PROFESSOR (QUIETLY, IN SHOCK)(CONT'D)
Too late...

He gently lays O'KELLY's ARM on the BED, stands up slowly, and steps back, his gaze fixed on the body. The NURSE checks O'KELLY in vain, while the ORDERLY shakes his head—there's nothing more they can do.

The camera lingers on the PROFESSOR´s stunned face, and the scene fades out.

INT. PROFESSOR'S ROOM – DAY

ALICE (38), STEVE (42), and DANIEL LIVINGSTON (72) remain seated facing the PROFESSOR (90+) in his WHEELCHAIR by the WINDOW. The PROFESSOR seems drained, as though his story has sapped all his energy. He slumps momentarily but musters the strength to sit upright again, trembling with resolve.

PROFESSOR (TIRED, RESOLUTE)
O'Kelly's death marked the clinic's end. Looking back, it should have closed much sooner. But... even after   he was buried, people kept disappearing, right up until it finally shut down.

He hesitates, as if about to reveal a long-held secret.

PROFESSOR (WEAKLY) (CONT'D)

There's something I've never told anyone. The night
O'Kelly died... something happened to me. Part
of... his curse passed to me.

DANIEL, ALICE, and STEVE share alarmed glances. ALICE leans forward, her voice
quivering with shock.

ALICE (DISMAYED)
What... does that mean? How?

PROFESSOR (ALMOST WHISPERING)

I sense when something terrible

happens in that old clinic. And... in some horrific way,
I benefit from it. How else could I have lived this
long? And why else would I feel younger after
each... episode? It's like... the demon feeds on the
souls of the missing, and grants   us—his unwilling
servants—some piece of that stolen life.

ALICE widens her eyes, realizing that DENNIS, TOM, and now PAUL have likely
been caught in this unholy trap. She can barely breathe, tears forming.

ALICE (DESPERATE, VOICE TREMBLING)

 Then Dennis and Tom and Paul... they disappeared in that clinic
because

of this curse? How... how do we get them back?

STEVE, noticing ALICE is on the verge of collapse, gently places a hand on her
shoulder.

STEVE (SOFTLY)

Alice... we'll figure something out.

The PROFESSOR shakes his head, looking worn to the core. DANIEL reaches to
steady him.

PROFESSOR (WEAK, REMORSEFUL)

I don't know. I don't know what becomes of them in the
end. One

life for another. That demon… or whatever it is… consumes their souls, and forces its power upon us without our asking. It sounds insane, but I have no other explanation.

(He pauses, struggling to breathe)

I'm so tired. I just want to sleep… never wake up. Now I understand O'Kelly. I'm sorry, Daniel… Alice… Steve. None of you deserve this.

He turns his WHEELCHAIR toward the WINDOW, tears streaking his face. DANIEL gently rests a hand on his father's shoulder, unsure how to comfort him.

STEVE (QUIETLY, TO ALICE)

Let's give him some space, Alice.

ALICE, still shell-shocked and overcome with pity, nods and stands. STEVE takes her hand, guiding her toward the DOOR. DANIEL stays with the PROFESSOR, who sobs quietly into the silence.

They close the DOOR softly behind them, leaving DANIEL and the PROFESSOR a-lone. The camera lingers on the closed door as faint sounds of grief recede into silence.

EXT. IN FRONT OF THE PROFESSOR'S HOUSE – DAY

The sun is higher in the sky as ALICE (38) and STEVE (42) sit in STEVE'S CAR. In the background, the PROFESSOR'S old yet well-kept HOUSE is visible. Neither has fully closed their doors yet, and the windows are slightly rolled down, letting in the ambient sound of birds chirping.

ALICE (VOICE TREMBLING)

I still can't believe what we just heard, Steve. This curse… how it's affected people from the clinic. I want answers, even if… even if there's barely any hope left for Dennis. I need to know.

She falls silent, struggling to maintain her composure.

STEVE (SOFTLY)

Alice, I get it—you need to do something. But who's going to believe us? The mayor'll laugh in our faces, the chief won't even listen, and the town'll think we're insane.

ALICE (RESOLUTE)

Then let them. I'm not quitting, not after everything
I've seen and heard. I need certainty, Steve. Even if
I find out there's nothing more I can do... at least I'll
know where I stand.

STEVE exhales deeply, looks at ALICE. He sees the fierce determination in her
eyes.

STEVE (SINCERELY)

I never imagined, when this started, that I'd meet someone
who'd fight this hard. You've changed, Alice—and I respect
that more than I can say.

ALICE (INTENTLY)

So you're with me on this now?

STEVE (HESITATES, THEN RELENTS)

I can see you're serious. You'd do anything to figure this out.
I just never expected we'd be in something this... beyond be-
lief.

(short pause)

Alright. Let's go back to town for now, catch our breath... then
figure out the next step.

ALICE nods, still tense with determination, but agrees to STEVE'S plan.

ALICE (HALF WHISPERING)

Okay. Let's go.

They both close their car doors. STEVE starts the ENGINE, and the CAR moves off
slowly. A tense silence settles between

them--a mixture of determination, exhaustion, and a faint glimmer of hope.

EXT. ABANDONED PSYCHIATRIC CLINIC – FRONT OF THE CLINIC – EVE-
NING

Several CARS are parked on the overgrown FORECOURT of the old clinic. Young pe-

110

ople get out, greeting each other boisterously and hauling party supplies into the building: CRATES of drinks, a portable GRILL, boxes of food, a MIXING CONSOLE, and a GENERATOR. From one car, MUSIC is already blaring, prompting some of the teens to dance and shout.

Another CAR pulls up and joins the others. TRACY (17) and AMELIA ABRAHAM (18) step out, immediately surrounded by other young people who enthusiastically congratulate AMELIA ABRAHAM on her birthday.

TEENS (OVERLAPPING)

Hey AMELIA ABRAHAM, happy birthday! / This is gonna be the party of the century! / What a cool spot, right?

AMELIA ABRAHAM looks a bit uneasy, glancing toward the abandoned CLINIC. She hesitates briefly.

AMELIA ABRAHAM (QUIETLY TO TRACY)

If my dad knew we were partying here... he'd kill me.

TRACY (LAUGHING, WRAPPING AN ARM AROUND AMELIA ABRAHAM)

Don't worry! It's the perfect   spot—old and spooky. Guaranteed to be unforgettable.

A few TEENS nod in agreement. The festive energy rubs off on AMELIA ABRAHAM, who smiles timidly but soon gets caught up in the excitement.

TEEN 1

Relax, AMELIA ABRAHAM. We'll make sure nothing goes wrong.

AMELIA ABRAHAM (HESITANT, THEN DETERMINED)

All right... I guess I don't want to be a buzzkill.

A low RUMBLE sounds as someone inside starts the GENERATOR. Soon, LIGHT flickers on in several WINDOWS of the second floor. A strong MUSIC BASS begins thumping, gently shaking the walls.

TRACY (GRINNING)

Sounds like the party's started!

Cheering, the group heads inside the CLINIC, laughing, dancing, and singing. AMELIA ABRAHAM takes a deep breath and finally follows, her initial unease fading beneath the party spirit.

EXT. MAIN STREET – DAY

Steeped in thought, STEVE (42) drives along the MAIN ROAD, his expression distant. ALICE (38), also lost in thought, gazes out the passenger-side window. They pass a HOMELESS MAN pushing a heavily loaded SHOPPING CART along the sidewalk. The cart overflows with BOTTLES, CARDBOARD, CLOTHES, and random items salvaged from the trash. A BRIGHT RED BACKPACK hangs on the side.

ALICE (SUDDENLY SHOUTING)

Stop right now!

Startled, STEVE slams on the brakes, TIRES squealing as the CAR skids to a halt.

ALICE yanks open the door, hastily unclips her SEATBELT, and jumps out. STEVE watches her in astonishment.

ALICE rushes toward the HOMELESS MAN, grabbing at the RED BACKPACK. Spooked, the man ducks behind his CART, then leaps forward to defend his "property."

HOMELESS MAN (ANGRY)
Hands off! That's mine!

ALICE (UPSET)

This is my son's backpack!

They tussle over the BACKPACK, shouting at each other. STEVE hurries over, trying to defuse the situation.

STEVE (FIRM BUT CALM)

Stop, both of you! I'm a police officer.

He shows the HOMELESS MAN his BADGE. The man hesitates, still distrustful. ALICE stands there, breathing heavily, ready to pounce again.

112

STEVE (TO THE HOMELESS MAN) (CONT'D)

We don't want trouble. Just let me see the backpack, okay?

Reluctantly, the HOMELESS MAN hands the BACKPACK to STEVE. ALICE snatches
it away from him, unzips it despite the man's protests.

ALICE (BREATHLESS, POINTING INSIDE)
Look—Dennis's name and address are

on this tag!

Tears fill her eyes as she clutches the BAG.

ALICE (ANGUISHED, TO THE HOMELESS MAN)
(CONT'D)

Where did you get it? What did you do with
Dennis?

The HOMELESS MAN raises his arms in defense, stammering.

HOMELESS MAN

I-I just found it! Over by the old clinic. I called
out, nobody answered. Didn't steal it, I
swear! If it's so important to you, keep it... I
don't want trouble with the cops.

STEVE (REASSURING, TO ALICE)

Calm down, Alice. It seems he really knows nothing.

The HOMELESS MAN looks at them pleadingly, then steps back, grasping
his CART and hurrying away. ALICE rummages through the BAG, recognizing every piece of clothing, each item definitely belonging to DENNIS. Tears
roll down her cheeks.

ALICE (TEARFUL)

It's all his... he's gone. I... I'll never see
him again.

STEVE places a comforting hand on her shoulder and pulls her into a gentle
hug. The HOMELESS MAN seizes the moment to shuffle off with his cart.
STEVE nods to him silently to leave.

                    STEVE (QUIETLY TO
          ALICE) I'm so sorry…

                    ALICE (WEAKLY)

     At least I know he was really at the clinic.

STEVE nods, carefully guides ALICE—and her newly found

BAG—back to the CAR. He closes her DOOR, then goes around to get in himself. The ENGINE starts, and they drive off with ALICE gripping the BACK-
PACK tightly in her arms.

INT./EXT. STEVE'S CAR – DAY

ALICE (38) sits in the passenger seat, clutching DENNIS' bright RED BACKPACK as
if it's her lifeline. She stares out the WINDSHIELD, her eyes distant and filled with a
dawning realization. STEVE (42) casts worried glances her way while navigating the
ROAD.

For a moment, neither speaks until STEVE breaks the tense silence softly.

                    STEVE (QUIETLY, CAREFULLY)
          Alice… are you all right? Can I do anything?

ALICE turns to him slowly. Her voice is calm yet charged with profound despair.

                    ALICE (CALM BUT RESOLUTE)

          Am I all right? No, Steve. Not at all. But… (holds up the
          BACKPACK) …isn't this enough?

STEVE furrows his brow, not immediately grasping her meaning.

                    ALICE (LOUDER, ANGUISHED) (CONT'D)

          Is this backpack not proof enough that something
          terrible has happened? That Dennis… (she
          swallows) …this is his bag, Steve. He… he's…

STEVE closes his eyes briefly, coming to grips with what it signifies. His own last
threads of hope fray.

                              114

                    STEVE (SADLY)

        Yeah… it's enough. More than enough. Unfortunately.

ALICE lowers her gaze to the BACKPACK, tears forming. She quickly blinks them
away, drawing a shaky breath.

                ALICE (SUDDENLY DETERMINED)

        All right. Then take me to the station. I´m done waiting
        around...

        I want this damned town to wake up, and if I have to pres-
        sure every last person, so be it.

STEVE swallows hard, sensing her iron resolve.

                    STEVE (SOFTLY)

        You sure about this?

ALICE nods, her expression set.

                        ALICE

        Yes. Drive me to the station.

STEVE hesitates a second, giving her a searching look. Then he presses down on the
GAS PEDAL, accelerating. The camera lingers on ALICE, gripping the BACKPACK
even tighter, as she focuses on the road ahead---ready for the next step.

INT. ABANDONED PSYCHIATRIC CLINIC – EVENING

What used to be dark HALLWAYS and ROOMS in the old clinic now pulse with the beat
of thumping MUSIC. A small GENERATOR hums in the corridor, drowned out by the
pounding BASS from an improvised DJ setup. Several FLOODLIGHTS and COLORFUL
LIGHTS splash the walls, transforming dusty decay into a vibrant party atmosphere.

AMELIA ABRAHAM (18) and TRACY (17) stand by the DJ CONSOLE, where a TEEN
in headphones is mixing tracks. Teens are dancing, laughing, clinking PLASTIC CUPS
together, and raiding COOLERS of DRINKS. The energy is high, and any former worries about the old clinic are all but forgotten.

                    AMELIA ABRAHAM (SMILING, RAISING HER CUP)

        I can't believe this is my birthday party... It's incre-
        dible!

                    TRACY (GRINNING, TOASTING WITH HER)

        Told you I had something epic planned. (glances around)

        Could there be a better place for the party of the year?

AMELIA ABRAHAM nods enthusiastically, clinking cups with TRACY. A COUPLE
OF GUYS join them, raising cups to AMELIA ABRAHAM in another birthday cheer.

                    GUY 1 (SHOUTING OVER THE BASS)
        Happy eighteenth!

                    GUY 2

        Dude, this party's insane!

AMELIA ABRAHAM smiles widely, her face glowing with happiness. The booming MU-
SIC, the vibrant LIGHTS, and all her FRIENDS make her forget any earlier nerves. She
dances a few steps, then takes a gulp from her cup. Time seems to pause in this moment of unbridled joy.

                    TRACY (TEASINGLY, WINKING)

         Come on, we gotta see Jonas. He's grilling in the next
        room.

                    AMELIA ABRAHAM (LAUGHING)
        That's guaranteed to be awesome!

They weave through the dancing crowd, the CLINIC'S ROOMS lit up with bright, swirling colors. Outside, the night sky has nearly taken over, leaving only the artificial
LIGHT and the relentless MUSIC filling the scene.

INT. POLICE STATION – DAY

ALICE (38) bursts through the station's SWINGING DOORS, clutching DENNIS' red
BACKPACK tightly. She strides purposefully toward the corridor ahead. A YOUNG
OFFICER at the front desk tries to intercept her, but stops when STEVE (42) enters
right behind her.

                    OFFICER (UNSURE)
          Steve— uh, Inspector Miles?

                    STEVE (CURTLY)

     It's fine, let her through.

He rushes after ALICE, who heads straight for the HANK OBAMA'S OFFICE and
flings the DOOR open without knocking.

INT. HANK OBAMA'S OFFICE – CONTINUOUS

The CHIEF (HANK OBAMA, 62) recoils from his DESK, startled, as ALICE barges in
and slams the BACKPACK onto his cluttered workspace. Several items clatter to the
floor.

                    HANK OBAMA (ANGRY)

     What the hell is this? Have you lost your mind?

                    ALICE (RAISING HER VOICE)

          I've had enough! This backpack is the final proof Dennis
          and Tom were here—and that they're NOT just going to
          turn up somewhere like you all keep insisting!

STEVE enters, slightly out of breath, as the CHIEF tries to defend himself.

                    HANK OBAMA

          Ms. Walker, I can't help it if—

                    ALICE (CUTTING HIM OFF SHARPLY)

          Oh, but you can. You could've done something for years!
          Instead, you let people vanish again and again. My son…
          Tom… Paul… And this so-called professor has been ignored
          all this time!

                    HANK OBAMA (RED-FACED)
          That's out of order—!

ALICE pounds the DESK with her free hand, still clutching the BACKPACK.

STEVE attempts to calm her, but ALICE plows on, voice quivering with anger and grief.

ALICE

You've done NOTHING all these years! Your inaction cost lives—my son's life. How many more have to disappear before you finally do something?

The CHIEF blanches, shouting at STEVE:

HANK OBAMA

Miles! Get her out of here, now! This is trespassing and a direct insult to my authority!

STEVE (FIRMLY)

Chief, I'm not doing that. Alice is right—this whole town is in denial. If people don't wake up, every death is on their conscience.

Several OFFICERS peek in from the corridor, drawn by the commotion. A few nod in agreement, others slip away, not wanting any trouble.

Realizing he's losing control, the CHIEF forces himself to calm down. He lowers his voice, trying to shift the blame.

HANK OBAMA

Look… it's not my fault. The mayor's the one who keeps shutting everything down. I—

ALICE (INTERRUPTING)

Shame on you! Always blaming someone else instead of showing some backbone!

Just then, the PHONE on the DESK rings. Everyone pauses. The CHIEF grabs the receiver, still fuming.

HANK OBAMA
Obama—

An angry, muffled voice can be heard— it's the MAYOR, apparently yelling down the line.

HANK OBAMA (PALING) (CONT'D)

Mr. Mayor, I—

(hearing something shocking)

A… a newspaper article tomorrow? You can't
just—!

He stammers as the MAYOR seemingly fires him on the spot. Then a harsh click
indicates the call is cut off. A heavy silence falls as the CHIEF lowers the phone,
stunned.

HANK OBAMA (FURIOUS) (CONT'D)

Dammit all!

He slams the RECEIVER onto the DESK, which tumbles to the floor. With trembling
hands, he snatches his JACKET from the coat hook.

HANK OBAMA (CONT'D)

Fine! Do whatever you want. I'm done with this
town! All these years I've been good enough—
now this.

He storms past ALICE, STEVE, and the bewildered OFFICERS into the hallway. No one
moves as he stomps out. From outside the doorway, one might see him charge angrily
toward the exit.

ALICE remains there, hugging the BACKPACK, tears streaming down her face. She
sinks onto the CHAIR in front of the HANK OBAMA'S empty DESK, her voice trembling.

ALICE (SOFTLY, TO STEVE)

What's happening? What do we do now? Is everything
against me?

Tears roll down her cheeks, and STEVE averts his gaze, equally at a loss for words.
A heavy silence settles in the chaotic office.

INT. ABANDONED PSYCHIATRIC CLINIC – LATE EVENING

MUSIC thunders through the CORRIDORS and the makeshift-decorated ROOMS. Next door, where the GENERATOR hums, many TEENS are still partying hard, dancing and yelling with drinks in hand.

AMELIA ABRAHAM (18) and TRACY (17) aren't in the main dance area, but in the AD-JACENT ROOM, where a GRILL has been set up. HUNGRY TEENS crowd around the grill, while one TEEN in an apron is flipping burgers for everyone.

TEEN AT THE GRILL (LOUD, CHEERFUL)

Anyone still need a burger? Come on, I've got plenty!

Calls of "Here! Me!" compete with the booming MUSIC. Suddenly, a GIRL stumbles in, crying and screaming. She's disheveled, wearing only some hastily thrown-on clothes. Her whole body trembles with fear.

The TEENS gathered around the grill turn down the MUSIC a notch, but in the NEXT ROOM, it remains so loud that the GIRL's screams are nearly drowned out.

A TEEN (CONCERNED)

Hey, what's wrong? Are you okay?

THE GIRL (SOBBING)

He… he… George… we… oh god…

ANOTHER TEEN (QUESTIONING)
What about George? Did he do something to you? Did
he hurt you?

The GIRL shakes her head, hand trembling as she brushes her hair back. She's terrified and shaking uncontrollably.

THE GIRL (STAMMERING)

No… some… thing… just grabbed him and took him a-
way… I don't know what it was. A dog? Or a wolf? …God,
I'm so scared…

A hushed murmur spreads through the group. Some TEENS look horrified; others think it's a joke.

A TEEN (LOUDLY)

We've gotta find George! Come on, guys!

A small group of BOYS abandons their burgers and rushes into the CORRIDOR, headed toward the darker ROOMS to look for George. The frightened GIRL still stands there, half-naked and trembling.

At this point, AMELIA ABRAHAM dances into the room, still lighthearted from music and maybe drinks. She stops short when she sees the distraught GIRL now collapsed on the FLOOR.

AMELIA ABRAHAM (ALARMED, KNEELING BE-SIDE HER)

Oh my God, what happened?

The TEENS around them shrug or shake their heads, clueless.

A TEEN

We're not sure. She says something grabbed George, carried him off. A few of the guys went to check.

AMELIA ABRAHAM looks at the GIRL, who sobs quietly, face down. In the distance, the BASS still pounds away, while the rest of the party next door remains oblivious to the incident.

INT. PROFESSOR'S ROOM – DAY

A dim glow filters through the curtains. THE PROFESSOR (90+) lies in BED, frail, already showing the first signs of a SEIZURE. His body convulses slightly, half closed EYES fluttering, and occasional MOANS escaping his lips. On a small TABLE by the bed are neatly arranged SYRINGES and MEDICINES—neat in what little order the chaos allows.

DANIEL LIVINGSTON (72) enters quietly, immediately recognizing another seizure has started.

DANIEL (CONCERNED)

Father… can you hear me? I'm here.

The PROFESSOR's spasms intensify, tossing him from side to side. DANIEL rushes to the bed, speaking soothingly, but the spasms worsen.

>   DANIEL (IMPLORING) (CONT'D)
>
>   Stay calm, it'll be all right. I'll help you.

He grabs a SYRINGE, quickly drawing MEDICATION and injecting it into the PROFES-
SOR's UPPER ARM. He must grip the PROFESSOR's arm firmly, struggling against
the violent tremors. Finished, he places the syringe aside, breathing a sigh of relief.

>   DANIEL (RELIEVED) (CONT'D)
>
>   This should take effect soon… You'll sleep,
>   like always.

With shaky hands, DANIEL tidies the ROOM. He props the old WHEELCHAIR upright
by the WINDOW, picks up a fallen PILLOW. Suddenly, he hears a horrifying MOAN
from the BED. The PROFESSOR's convulsions flare up again, more extreme than before.

>   DANIEL (ALARMED) (CONT'D)
>
>   No… that's not right. The medication should
>   have worked!

The PROFESSOR arches his BACK, his EYES and facial VEINS turning a sinister
BLACK. He mumbles strange, ominous sounds. His entire BODY thrashes so violently
the BED rattles.

>   DANIEL (TREMBLING, PANICKED) (CONT'D)
>
>   Father! Please—stay with me!

Frantically, he readies a second SYRINGE, drawing another dose of the drug. His
hands shake so much he nearly spills it. Finally, he manages, half-throwing himself
onto the PROFESSOR to administer the injection.

>   DANIEL (PANTING) (CONT'D)
>
>   Forgive me… I have to do this!

Once the second dose is injected, the PROFESSOR collapses back onto the BED
with a choked groan, his MUSCLES slackening. But DANIEL notices his wild, darting EYE MOVEMENTS, as though the PROFESSOR is trapped in a dire nightmare.

DANIEL (QUAVERING) (CONT'D)

Oh God… what have I done?

He pulls the BLANKET over the PROFESSOR and gently strokes his forehead. Then he glances at the now-empty SYRINGE in his hand. Looking over the MEDICATION'S INSTRUCTIONS from the IV stand, he eventually finds the dosage warnings, his face draining of color as he reads.

DANIEL (WHISPERING) (CONT'D)

Another injection… would kill him.

Stricken with indecision and fear, he sits on the edge of the BED, still clutching the empty SYRINGE in his trembling fingers. The PROFESSOR breathes shallowly, softly whimpering as the drug's effect overwhelms him. DANIEL just stares, overwhelmed, uncertain, yet resolved not to risk another fatal mistake.

INT. ABANDONED PSYCHIATRIC CLINIC – ROOM – NIGHT

A dimly lit ROOM with a worn-out MATTRESS on the floor, covered by a BLANKET. It's the makeshift "cozy corner" where GEORGE and his date had been. A weak LIGHT near the door barely illuminates the front area, leaving the back WALLS in shadow.

Three TEENAGE BOYS (BOY 1, BOY 2, BOY 3) enter in a hurry.

BOY 1 (CALLING)

George? Hey, man, you all right?

BOY 2 (LOOKING AROUND)

He's not here. Where'd he go?

They check the blanket, glance around, but find no sign of GEORGE. BOY 3 spots a FLASHLIGHT on the floor and picks it up, switching it on. Its stronger beam sweeps the room's corners. Suddenly, he freezes.

BOY 3 (STARTLED, WHISPERING)

Uh… guys? Get over here. What the hell is that?

He directs the LIGHT at the WALL, revealing BLACK, VEIN-LIKE GROWTHS sprea-ding along it, glistening with a wet sheen, seeming to move slowly outward.

BOY 2 (UNEASY)

Damn… that's creepy. The heck is it?

BOY 1 takes a step closer, hesitantly touching one of these "veins." Some slimy SUB-STANCE clings to his fingers. He rubs it between thumb and forefinger.

BOY 1 (DISGUSTED)
Ugh… what is this slime?

He turns to show the others, trying to fling off the black ooze. In that moment, a monstrous, nightmarish CLAW shoots out from the darkness, grabbing his HEAD.

BOY 1 (SCREAMING) (CONT'D)

Aaaah—!

He's violently yanked back into the SHADOW, his scream abruptly cut off. BOY 2 and BOY 3 shout in terror, momentarily paralyzed by what they've witnessed.

BOY 2 (PANICKED)
Holy— RUN!

They dash toward the DOOR, shrieking. The second they reach the CORRIDOR, BOY 3 feels something latch onto his

LEG—something drags him down. He lands hard and is pulled back into the ROOM, screaming. His eyes lock onto BOY 2, wide with desperation.

BOY 3 (PLEADING)

H-help!

His EYES go wide, turning BLACK in seconds. A choking GURGLE escapes him, as if drowning in his own blood. Then he's swallowed by the darkness within the ROOM.

BOY 2, having escaped into the HALL, casts one horrified look back. He only glimpses BOY 3's now blackened stare before it vanishes into the gloom. With a final, desperate cry, BOY 2 bolts down the corridor, frantically yelling for help as he flees toward the lit area.

INT. ABANDONED PSYCHIATRIC CLINIC – ROOM WITH GRILL – NIGHT

Music pounds, bass shaking the walls. Some TEENS dance, others lie exhausted or tipsy in corners. A few are still grilling burgers when suddenly a BOY bursts in, panic-stricken.

BOY (YELLING, FRANTIC)

Something's here! It—it wants to kill us all!

Startled faces whip around, the MUSIC still blaring. One GIRL, realizing the meaning of his words, screams in terror and bolts into the HALL. Her shriek echoes, cut short as she's yanked away by something invisible.

SEVERAL TEENS (TERRIFIED)

Oh God, what—?

/ Where did she go?!

Panic erupts. Everyone rushes about, some heading for the NEXT ROOM where the music is playing. CRATES and DRINKS spill, the GRILL topples over with a loud hiss of fire. The sound system is knocked over in the mayhem, abruptly silencing the MUSIC. Only the GENERATOR'S rattle and panicked shouting remain.

INT. ABANDONED PSYCHIATRIC CLINIC – ADJACENT ROOM WITH MUSIC EQUIPMENT – SAME TIME

AMELIA ABRAHAM (18), TRACY (17), and others stand in confusion as the fleeing TEENS storm in, screaming and clinging to one another. Within seconds, panic spreads here as well.

VARIOUS TEENS

Run! There's something in the hallway!

/ It's dragging people into the dark!

Objects scatter, the MUSIC SYSTEM crashes to the floor, going silent. Through the chaos, a sinister MURMUR grows steadily louder.

AMELIA ABRAHAM (GRABBING TRACY'S ARM)
Come on, we have to get out of here!

She pulls TRACY into the CORRIDOR, where the weak LIGHT flickers ominously. In the dimness, bizarre SHAPES emerge from the shadows. A monstrous CLAW snatches a TEEN, who screams as he's yanked backward into the DARK.

TRACY (SCREAMING)

Oh God, what is that?!

AMELIA ABRAHAM (PANICKED)

I don't know, just run!

They sprint toward the STAIRWAY, joined by a crowd of terrified TEENS. Claws dart out from the shadows to grab arms or legs, echoing shrieks filling the old, deserted halls. The LAST of the group stumble, pulled into the GLOOM. AMELIA ABRAHAM and TRACY tumble down the STAIRS to the GROUND FLOOR, sheer terror in their eyes.

INT. PROFESSOR'S ROOM – NIGHT

A faint, dim LIGHT spills through the curtains. THE PROFESSOR (90+) lies in his BED, wracked by severe convulsions. Black, throbbing veins spider around his EYES, and incomprehensible, dark sounds issue from his MOUTH. His SON, DANIEL (72), stands at the bedside, desperately trying to restrain him.

DANIEL (PLEADING, PANICKED)
Father… please… calm down! I… I

can't take this anymore!

The PROFESSOR emits a low, guttural growl and grips DANIEL by the THROAT with startling force, choking the breath out of him.

DANIEL (CHOKING, DESPERATE) (CONT'D)

F-Father… let me… go!

His hands frantically paw at the NIGHTSTAND, searching for the INFUSION SYRINGE. The PROFESSOR throws his HEAD back, his entire BODY shaking wildly, uttering bestial, incoherent noises.

With a final burst of strength, DANIEL snatches the SYRINGE, yanks off the CAP, and plunges it into the PROFESSOR'S NECK. He depresses the plunger fully, his own vision edging with darkness as his father's grip tightens on his throat.

DANIEL (GASPING) (CONT'D)

F-forgive me, Father…

126

The PROFESSOR lets out a roar as the MEDICATION floods his system. His hold on DANIEL slackens. DANIEL staggers back, coughing and gulping air. The SYRINGE falls to the floor with a rattle.

DANIEL (PANTING, TREMBLING) (CONT'D)

God… what have I done?

The PROFESSOR'S EYES flicker, his BODY convulsing in one last frantic seizure. DANIEL realizes with horror that this dose might be lethal. In despair, he grabs a PILLOW from the foot of the BED.

DANIEL (SOBBING) (CONT'D)

I'm so sorry…

The PROFESSOR emits a feeble gargle, the black discoloration around his eyes and veins looking dreadful and unnatural. DANIEL squeezes his own eyes shut, tears coursing down his cheeks.

DANIEL (CRYING OUT IN ANGUISH) (CONT'D)

Forgive me, Father!

He presses the PILLOW over the PROFESSOR'S FACE with all his remaining strength, tears strangling his voice as he suffocates his dying father. The PROFESSOR'S ragged sounds weaken, then fade. In his final twitch, DANIEL feels life slip away from the old man.

At last, DANIEL collapses, overcome, onto the lifeless body. Clutching the PILLOW, he sobs uncontrollably, his anguished cries echoing in the stillness of the ROOM.

INT. ABANDONED PSYCHIATRIC CLINIC – CORRIDOR – NIGHT

A dimly lit HALLWAY, now nearly overtaken by PULSATING BLACK, VEIN-LIKE GROWTHS crawling across the WALLS. AMELIA ABRAHAM (18) runs alongside TRACY (17) and a handful of other TEENS, all fleeing in terror. Their FOOTSTEPS echo, accompanied by frantic breaths and chaotic screams.

TRACY (SHRIEKING)

AMELIA ABRAHAM, run faster!

One TEEN trips over some RUBBLE or decaying object on the floor and goes down. His SCREAM abruptly cuts off as a HORRIFIC SHADOWY FIGURE yanks him into the darkness. From the gloom comes a DEMENTED MURMUR, like commands issued in an unknown tongue.

> AMELIA ABRAHAM (DESPERATELY, ON PHONE)
> Dad… please, help us… We're in the
>
> old clinic… hurry…!

The CALL is fraught with static, AMELIA ABRAHAM's VOICE trembling. As she speaks, in the rush of people pushing past each other, the PHONE is knocked from her hand or lost in the scuffle. The MAYOR's concerned voice briefly echoes, then a CRASH as the PHONE hits the floor and disappears beneath stamping feet.

> AMELIA ABRAHAM (ANGUISHED)(CONT'D)
>
> No! Damn it, my phone…!

> DEMONIC VOICE (FROM THE DARKNESS, UN-
> INTELLIGIBLE)
>
> Deep, hissed words like commands

The TEENS scream anew when another CLAW darts out of the SHADOWS, dragging yet another person away with a blood-curdling shriek.

> TRACY (SOBBING)
>
> We have to get out of here, now!

AMELIA ABRAHAM and the others bolt, desperately shoving through the HALL. Scattered debris—bottles, crates, shattered furniture—litters the floor. The BLACK VEINS on the WALLS flicker ominously with each passing glint of LIGHT, as if drawn to the fleeing TEENS.

At last, they see the double doors of the MAIN ENTRANCE. Those who remain burst through them, stumbling into the NIGHT. Outside, the cool air offers momentary relief from the suffocating horror within.

AMELIA ABRAHAM stumbles onto the FRONT STOOP, back turned to the clinic, gazing in terror at the gloom behind her. Faint SCREAMS echo from within, punctuated by that eerie MURMUR and the final, frantic cries of those still trapped.

INT. POLICE STATION – EVENING

A handful of OFFICERS stand in a loose circle, including STEVE (42) and ALICE (38).

The atmosphere is tense yet tinged with a new sense of purpose since HANK OBAMA left abruptly. Another OFFICER gently closes the now-empty HANK OBAMA's office door.

                    STEVE (RESOLUTELY)

        Look, we all know something terrible is happening. All
        these disappearances the town's been ignoring, including
        Alice's son Dennis and his friend Tom… we've turned a
        blind eye for too long.

He scans the group, clearing his throat briefly. ALICE is seated off to the side, head bowed, clutching DENNIS' BACKPACK near her.

                STEVE (CONTINUING) (CONT'D)

        The professor has been telling us unbelievable stuff:
        a curse, a demon that devours people. Sounds
        crazy, sure. But Dennis' backpack alone is proof
        enough that we can't keep dismissing this. We have
        to act now, whether the business community likes it
        or not.

                    AN OFFICER (QUIETLY)

        Yeah… we've been ignoring this far too long.

Murmurs of agreement ripple through the OFFICERS.

                        STEVE (FIRM)

        So let's put together a plan. We need to find out
        what's really going on and start protecting pe-
        ople. We can't keep pretending it's none of our
        business.

Some of the OFFICERS start discussing strategy, pulling out maps and notes. ALICE, throughout, sits on a CHAIR apart from the group, lost in her own thoughts. STEVE no-tices her distant look and walks over. He kneels beside her, gently placing his hands on hers.

                STEVE (SOFTLY) (CONT'D)

        Alice… I know this is hard for you. But we're finally
        getting somewhere. We've got backup, we—

                ALICE (QUIET, BITTER) What's the

point? Dennis is dead. Nothing we do now will
bring him back… so what does it matter?

She lifts her gaze, tears shimmering in her eyes. STEVE exhales and presses
her hands gently.

STEVE (SOFT)

Maybe we can at least keep it from happening to
anyone else. And who knows… we might still find
some answers.

Right then, the STATION DOOR slams open, revealing the MAYOR (DONALD ABRA-
HAM, 53) rushing in with his WIFE (LILLIAN ABRAHAM, 49). He's panting, clearly having run all the way.

MAYOR DONALD ABRAHAM (DESPERATE,
PLEADING)

Help! Please… my daughter—AMELIA ABRA-
HAM—she's in the old clinic! Something terrible's
happening, I know it. Her phone call… oh god!

LILLIAN ABRAHAM (TEAR-CHOKED)

She called, screaming, saying she

was at the old clinic, then the line went dead!

A hush falls over the OFFICERS. STEVE stands upright, ALICE jumps from her chair,
eyes wide. The OFFICERS snatch up their GEAR and JACKETS.

STEVE (LOUDLY, AUTHORITATIVE)

You heard him, folks. Let's move!

They sprint to the EXIT, ALICE close behind, shock etched on her face. MAYOR and
LILLIAN ABRAHAM lead the way, while OFFICERS and ALICE chase them. Outside,
they pile into their VEHICLES, engines roaring to life.

MAYOR DONALD ABRAHAM (FROM HIS CAR
WINDOW)

Please—save AMELIA ABRAHAM!

TIRES SQUEAL as the CONVOY of patrol cars and the mayor's vehicle speeds
off.

The last glimpse shows ALICE sitting alongside STEVE in his patrol car, still hugging DENNIS' BACKPACK tightly, staring into the night.

EXT. ABANDONED PSYCHIATRIC CLINIC – FRONT OF THE CLINIC – NIGHT

Cars screech to a halt, their HEADLIGHTS slicing through the darkness and illumina-ting a harrowing scene in front of the clinic. TEENAGERS, visibly traumatized, are sprawled across the driveway—some weeping on the ground, others clinging to one another. From the FIRST FLOOR windows, faint, flickering LIGHTS shine, and a dark, DEMONIC VOICE is audible all the way outside.

MAYOR DONALD ABRAHAM (53) jumps out of his car first, followed by his WIFE (49). He rushes toward the TEENS, frantically searching.

> MAYOR DONALD ABRAHAM (DESPERATE)
> AMELIA ABRAHAM?! AMELIA ABRAHAM?!

Where are you?!

Among the huddled YOUTHS, he finally spots AMELIA ABRAHAM (18), who's clearly in shock, holding onto TRACY (17). The moment she sees him, AMELIA ABRAHAM staggers into his arms, sobbing.

> AMELIA ABRAHAM (THROUGH TEARS)
> Dad… it was horrible…

The MAYOR clutches her tightly, his WIFE joining them. In the background, other OFFICERS—including STEVE (42)—and ALICE (38) step out of their vehicles and hurry to the TEENAGERS.

> STEVE (CONCERNED, TO A SMALL GROUP)

Did everyone get out? Is there anyone still inside?

The teens exchange unsure looks; some mumble shakily that they're not sure how many people there even were. Others whimper, too shocked to speak.

> ALICE (SCANNING THE CROWD)

No one knows if others might still   be in there?

The traumatized, vacant stares offer little hope. ALICE and STEVE share a grave look. The MAYOR remains kneeling by his daughter.

MAYOR DONALD ABRAHAM (RAISING HIS
HEAD, PLEADING)

Please… you have to check. There might still be
some inside…

A few OFFICERS nod at one another, forming a team. STEVE and ALICE join them, weapons drawn and flashlights at the ready, cautiously stepping through the MAIN ENT-RANCE, which is half open.

STEVE (QUIET, RESOLUTE)

Stay sharp. Eyes open.

The CAMERA shows the MAYOR, his WIFE, and the remaining TEENS watching fear-fully from outside. ALICE glances once more at AMELIA ABRAHAM and the MAYOR before vanishing into the CLINIC'S darkness.

EXT./INT. ABANDONED PSYCHIATRIC CLINIC – NIGHT

OUTSIDE:

Police cars and the teenagers' vehicles line the driveway, HEADLIGHTS casting beams across the grim scene. TEENS huddle, sobbing or clutching each other for comfort. From inside the clinic, a horrifying DEMONIC VOICE penetrates the night. The air is thick with crying and screams.

ENTRANCE HALL:

OFFICERS, including STEVE (42) and ALICE (38), cautiously move in with FLASH-LIGHTS and DRAWN GUNS. The voice inside is ear-splittingly loud, reverberating through the corridors. In the torch beams, ghastly SHAPES skitter at the edges of vision, each scuttling away or lurking at the boundaries.

FIRST ENCOUNTER:

One OFFICER spots a MONSTROUS FIGURE and, in fear, fires his weapon. The CREATURE recoils at the muzzle flash but soon reemerges, joined by others. The OFFICERS, seeing no effect from bullets, keep firing. A CREATURE grabs one OFFICER, yanking him screaming into the shadows. Realizing the fight is hopeless, the group retreats.

RETREAT:

They shoot wildly as they backtrack to the EXIT. Emerging breathless and shaken, they meet the TEENS, the MAYOR, and his WIFE outside. Fearful questions arise: "What happened? Why were you shooting?" STEVE explains that bullets don't seem to stop the creatures.

                    ALICE (EXHAUSTED, EYES WIDE)

        The professor said the demon's curse is bound to the cli-
        nic. They don't come outside—they fear the muzzle flas-
        hes. It's not the bullets, it's the fire.

                    A POLICE OFFICER (HESITANT)

        But we can't just… burn the place down! Who'll even
        go back in?

ALICE eyes the devastation, turning to see a GAS CAN on one TEEN'S TRUCK. She hoists it off the tailgate, sniffs, confirming it's gasoline.

                    ALICE (FIRM)

        Fire is the only option left.

She picks up a WOODEN SLAT, wraps a RAG around it, and pours a splash of gas onto the rag. She looks at STEVE.

                    ALICE (CONT'D)

        Light it.

STEVE, with reluctance, nods. He draws his ZIPPO lighter from a pocket.

                    STEVE (SOFTLY)

        Alright… but be careful.

ALICE grabs the GAS CAN and strides toward the ENTRANCE. Several OFFICERS protest, but she glares at them defiantly. STEVE follows her, brandishing the flaming torch to keep the creatures at bay.

                                        INSIDE THE HALL:

The moment ALICE and STEVE re-enter, shapes scuttle close. The DEMONIC MURMUR intensifies, as if sensing imminent threat. But the torch's flame drives the creatures back. ALICE and STEVE move deeper, pouring GASOLINE on floors and occasionally on walls, step by step retreating back toward the exit.

The eerie VOICE escalates into a vicious roar. Yet the monsters, hissing from the gloom, remain too frightened of the FLAME to attack directly. Reaching the ENTRANCE, ALICE tosses the nearly empty CAN into the main hall. More fuel splashes onto the wooden floor.

> ALICE (VOICE TREMBLING WITH ANGER)

This is for my son…

She meets STEVE'S eyes, who hands her the BURNING TORCH. ALICE hurls it into the room. Instantly, a whoosh of FLAME ignites, racing across the floor and up the walls. The CREATURES screech in agony as the fire spreads. The demonic voice crescendos in a final, dreadful shriek, then starts to wane.

ALICE and STEVE dash outside. The watchers on the lawn flinch as the flames burst through WINDOWS and cracks of the old building. They see the CLINIC interior being consumed by fire, the inhuman cries soon drowned by the roaring inferno.

At length, only the crackling flames remain. THE MAYOR DONALD ABRAHAM and LILLIAN ABRAHAM cling to their daughter, while traumatized TEENS cluster around, some crying, others numb. OFFICERS gather in silent shock.

STEVE wraps an arm around ALICE, who stands, eyes lowered in a mixture of grief, relief, and finality. The flames devour the building's dark secrets, and for now, the demon's threat is ended.

EXT. POLICE STATION – MORNING

It's a cool, sunny day. ALICE (38)'s CAR is parked in front of the station. STEVE (42) and ALICE stand together, the emotional weight of recent events hanging in the air. They both look exhausted, yet somehow relieved after the old clinic burned down and the demons—literal and figurative—were driven away.

> STEVE (QUIETLY, ALMOST APOLOGETIC)

I have to stay here, Alice. There's so much to do. It could take weeks, maybe months. The families, all the victims… And we can't really tell anyone the truth. Not in full.

> ALICE (WITH A FAINT SMILE)

I know. Officially, it was just a big fire. Everything else… they'll sweep it under the rug. Mold spores, hallucinations— that's how they'll explain it.

She sighs, tucking a stray strand of hair behind her ear. A light breeze passes by.

> STEVE (NODDING)
>
> It isn't fair. But we know what we know. And the
> main thing is the clinic can't hurt anyone anymore.

ALICE glances pensively at her trunk, recently closed, then looks back to STEVE.

> ALICE (SOFTLY)
>
> I need to get back to my world—my law office, all
> those files… without Dennis.
>
> > (her voice wavers)
>
> But I'm glad it's over. At least that much.

STEVE steps closer, placing a hand on her arm. He hesitates briefly, then pulls her into a gentle hug. For a moment, they stand there, mourning, grateful, and silently understanding one another.

> STEVE (SOFTLY)
>
> Things could have been different… for us.

> ALICE (WITH A SLIGHT, WISTFUL SMILE) Maybe in
> another time, another
>
> place. But not today.

A brief exchange of unspoken possibilities. Then ALICE pulls away slowly, opens the driver's door, and settles into the seat.

STEVE leans down to the open WINDOW.

> STEVE
>
> Drive safe, okay?
>
> > (beat)
>
> And keep in touch, please.

> ALICE (NODDING)
>
> I will. Promise.

(she starts the ENGINE)

Oh, and if you ever find my phone—I lost it back at
the clinic—bring it by, will you?

She gives STEVE a playful wink, shifts into GEAR, and eases out of the PARKING
SPOT. After rolling a yard or so, she stops and turns back to him.

ALICE (SMILING)(CONT'D)

Remember… if you find it.

STEVE (SMIRKING)

I won´t forget.

ALICE steps on the GAS, and the car heads off onto the road. STEVE watches it fade
around the bend, sighs quietly, then turns back toward the STATION entrance, hands in
his pockets, ready for the workload still awaiting him inside.

EXT. ABANDONED PSYCHIATRIC CLINIC – OUTSIDE THE BURNT-OUT CLI-
NIC – DAY

The CAMERA, close to the ground, slowly approaches the charred remains of the old
clinic. Smoke still drifts from the shattered WINDOWS. The sun casts a faint, ghostly
light on the devastated site.

A soft buzzing sound is heard—a PHONE on silent mode. As the CAMERA inches closer, the buzzing grows louder. The shot passes by the wreckage of the entrance, the
floor strewn with debris and ash.

Eventually, we notice something in the GRASS—nearly invisible—a SMART-
PHONE. Its SCREEN glows weakly, battery almost dead. As the CAMERA closes
in, the display reads:

"CALL FROM DENNIS"

The buzz intensifies momentarily, then there's a final BEEP as the battery dies. The
SCREEN goes dark, and the buzzing stops. For a moment, the CAMERA lingers on
the now-lifeless PHONE in the grass.

Then we cut to silence.

FADE TO BLACK.   END   CREDITS

Pitch Deck

TAGLINE

BLOG 2035 - *"Survival is just the beginning."*

LOGLINE

In a world devastated by relentless storms and ruthless crime lords, an ex-cop fights to protect his daughter and escape the ruins of civilization—before the next storm hits.

BRIEF SYNOPSIS

Tom Wagner, a former police officer, struggles to survive in a city ravaged by natural disasters and ruled by a criminal syndicate. As he fights to provide for his six-year-old daughter Sandra, he is forced into a cycle of dangerous under-the-table jobs. But when his friend, a local shopkeeper, is brutally murdered by crime boss Paul Klancy, Tom realizes that escape is the only way forward. With the help of his loyal neighbor Nancy, he must outwit Klancy's men, endure the next devastating storm, and carve a future beyond the city's ruins—before it's too late.

GENRE & TONE

- **Genre:** Post-apocalyptic Thriller, Survival Drama
- **Tone:** Dark, intense, and emotionally charged with moments of warmth and hope. A gritty, character-driven story about survival, sacrifice, and redemption.

TARGET AUDIENCE

- Fans of **gritty survival thrillers** and **post-apocalyptic dramas**.
- Viewers who appreciate **character-driven storytelling** with high emotional stakes.
- Ages **16-50**, with a focus on audiences who enjoyed *The Walking Dead, The Last of Us,* and *Mad Max: Fury Road.*

UNIQUE SELLING POINTS

1. **A grounded, post-apocalyptic setting** with a fresh twist—no zombies or nuclear war, just the brutal aftermath of unstoppable storms and the collapse of law and order.
2. **A gripping father-daughter dynamic**, similar to *The Last of Us,* driving the emotional core of the film.
3. **A strong, morally complex protagonist**—a man torn between survival and the values he once swore to uphold.
4. **A terrifying, charismatic villain** in Paul Klancy, who controls the city like a feudal warlord.
5. **A blend of high-stakes action and deep emotional storytelling**, balancing tension with heartfelt moments.

VISUAL CONCEPT

- **Cinematography:** Harsh, desaturated tones reflecting the city's decay; contrasting with warm, intimate lighting in moments of human connection.
- **World-building:** A city in ruins—collapsed buildings, makeshift markets, streets littered with debris, and Red Cross trucks collecting the dead.
- **Storms as a character:** Visually striking, with intense dust clouds, torrential rain, and eerie silence before destruction strikes.
- **Action sequences:** Realistic, brutal hand-to-hand combat, high-tension chases, and visceral survival moments.

KEY CHARACTERS

- **Tom Wagner (38, ex-cop, determined, emotionally scarred)** – A man haunted by his past, struggling to keep his daughter safe in a lawless world.
- **Sandra Wagner (6, innocent, resilient, hopeful)** – A child who represents the last piece of light in Tom's dark world.
- **Nancy (30, compassionate, strong-willed, survivor)** – The only person Tom truly trusts; she cares deeply for Sandra and hides her own painful past.
- **Paul Klancy (45, ruthless, charming, crime boss)** – A power-hungry warlord who rules the streets with fear and corruption.
- **Foo (75, wise, kind-hearted, shopkeeper)** – A symbol of the old world's values, murdered for standing up to Klancy.
- **Masters (40, conflicted, weary, police officer)** – An old ally of Tom's who knows the system is broken but is too afraid to fight back.

CONCLUSION / APPEAL

"Aftermath" isn't just another post-apocalyptic thriller—it's a deeply human story about survival, morality, and the fight for hope in a world on the brink. With **intense action, powerful emotions, and a cinematic world unlike any other**, this film will resonate with audiences craving gripping, character-driven narratives.

Tom Wagner's journey is more than survival—it's about redemption, love, and the will to fight back against the darkness.

Are you ready to bring *Aftermath* to life?

SCRIPT

BLOG 2035

Written by Frank Lehmann

First Draft 02.08.2025

Freiwasser Filmproduktion
Metelsdorfer Str. 2b
23972 Dorf Mecklenburg
GERMANY

Phone: +49 178 1339406
Mail: info@frank-lehmann.biz

EXT. CONNAUGHT PARK – DAY

The midday sun pierces through gray clouds, casting a fleeting warmth over Connaught Park. The air carries an unusual stillness, a fragile illusion of peace.

Parents and children scatter across the park, relishing the moment—as if the world outside wasn't crumbling.

Seated on a worn wooden bench, TOM WAGNER (38) flips through the pages of a dog-eared book, though his attention keeps drifting.

Nearby, SANDRA (6) swings high, her laughter crisp and pure against the surrounding ruins. Her joy is radiant, almost surreal in this world.

Beyond the park, piles of rubble tower, crumbling facades standing like forgotten ghosts of the past. Bulldozers churn through the wreckage, a grotesque symphony of destruction and survival.

Tom smiles wearily, watching Sandra wave at him from the creaky swing.

                    TOM (softly, to himself)
          Hold on to this joy.

His fingers tighten around the book, as if clinging to something fragile. His gaze lifts beyond the ruins, toward the distant harbor, where a broken skyline stretches across the horizon.

He takes a deep breath—

A moment of peace.

                    SUDDENLY—
          SIRENS SCREAM, ripping through the stillness.

The piercing ALARM freezes the park.

A STORM IS COMING.

PARENTS' FACES HARDEN. They snatch up their children, voices hushed but urgent. Sandra slows her swinging, turning to Tom, her face etched with fear.

SANDRA (small voice, unsure)

Dad... is it another storm?

Tom pushes to his feet, his eyes never leaving the horizon.

TOM   (calm bu firm)

It's alright, sweetheart. Come here.

He extends his hand.

Sandra rushes to him, slipping her tiny fingers into his.

Together, they move with the others, fear thick in the air. Bulldozers grind to a halt, workers abandoning their posts.

As the last stragglers disappear, the park falls silent,

the swing creaking emptily in the wind.

FADE OUT.

EXT. STREET – DAY

Tom tightens his grip on Sandra's hand as they hurry through the shattered streets.

RUBBLE litters the ground.

SIRENS WAIL.

THE WIND HOWLS.

The sky darkens—the storm draws closer.

Other passersby rush past them, eyes fixed ahead, driven by urgency.

NO ONE STOPS.

SUDDENLY—

An ELDERLY WOMAN stumbles.

She CRASHES to the pavement.

Others leap over her, barely glancing down.

Tom doesn't hesitate.

He releases Sandra's hand and rushes to her.

His grip is firm as he lifts her.

ELDERLY WOMAN(breathless, shaken)

Thank you... thank you.

She shoots a glance at the sky, fear flickering in her eyes. Without another word, she hurries away.

Tom grabs Sandra's hand again.

TOM (urgent but gentle)

Come on, we have to keep moving.

Sandra nods quickly, her wide eyes reflecting the storm's approach.

The wind roars louder, pulling at their clothes.

People disappear into shelters, the streets emptying fast.

The sirens echo through the hollow city.

FADE OUT.

EXT. BUILDING FRONT – DAY

Tom and Sandra reach their APARTMENT BUILDING.

The street is alive with urgency—people scramble for shelter, the storm's shadow looming.

Across the road, MR. FOO, one of the last shopkeepers, hurriedly locks up his store.

His hands shake. His movements are rushed.

PANICKED PASSERSBY dart past, their eyes hollow with dread.

Tom pauses at the entrance, scanning the street.

HE KNOWS NOT EVERYONE WILL MAKE IT.

                    TOM'S THOUGHTS (V.O.)
        Today, the truck collecting the dead will be full
        again.

His gaze meets MR. FOO'S.

A silent exchange of knowing—a brief nod of mutual understanding.

We'll survive. For now.

Tom pulls Sandra inside, the heavy door sealing them off from the chaos.

                                        FADE OUT.

INT. TOM'S APARTMENT – NIGHT

Tom locks the door with a heavy bolt, the metal clanking into place. A habit. A necessity.

Without hesitation, he moves through the apartment, closing the steel shutters, one by one. Outside, the wind howls, a creeping menace curling through the streets.

At the kitchen table, SANDRA (6) carefully sets up several candles, their small flames flickering, sending dancing shadows across the walls.

The power still holds, but they both know—when the storm fully arrives, it will fail. It always does.

KNOCK. KNOCK.

A sound at the door.

Tom stops mid-motion, his body tensing. His hand instinctively moves toward his belt—no gun. Not anymore.

He straightens, exhales, then steps toward the door, opening it just a crack.

NANCY (30) stands outside, a warm smile on her lips, a pot of soup cradled in her hands.

                    NANCY   (soft, reassuring)
          I thought a hot meal might be just what you need.

Tom nods, grateful, and steps aside. Nancy enters.

As soon as she's inside, Tom bolts the door behind her.

Nancy moves through the narrow hallway, placing the pot on the kitchen table. She turns to Sandra with a bright expression.

                    NANCY (CONT'D)
          (cheerful, motherly)   Hello, sweetheart!
          How was your day?

Sandra beams, eyes shining with the remnants of happiness.

                    SANDRA (excitedly, but with a hint of disappointment)

We went to the park! But then... the stupid storm
came. Again!

Nancy laughs softly, pulling Sandra into a comforting hug.

NANCY (gentle, soothing)

I'm sorry, sweetie. But you know what? We'll make
it cozy in here.

Tom watches them, a faint smile touching his lips. A fleeting moment of peace.

Then—

The shutters RATTLE, the wind pounding harder. The apartment trembles with the
storm's arrival.

Tom's smile fades.

He turns to the windows, his expression tightening.

TOM   (firm, but calm)

It's starting.

He strides toward a cabinet, opens it, and pulls out a board game.

Sets it on the table.

TOM (CONT'D) (soft, but determined)

Let's make the best of it.

Sandra nods enthusiastically, and Nancy casts Tom a quick, encouraging glance.

The storm rages outside, but inside, a fragile sense of security remains.

FADE OUT.

INT. TOM'S APARTMENT – KITCHEN – NIGHT

146

A game of LUDO is spread out on the table.

Tom, Sandra, and Nancy play intently, but Sandra bursts into laughter each time she moves a piece into the finish zone.

The storm outside is deafening.

The reinforced shutters tremble, but they hold.

The sound is relentless, a freight train barreling through the darkness.

Sandra's eyes flicker toward the windows, her small hands tightening into fists.

Tom notices.

He gently places his hand over hers.

> TOM (soothing, firm)
>
> It's alright, sweetheart. The storm can't reach us here.

Sandra nods, but the tension in her shoulders remains. She rolls the dice again.

Nancy smiles, knocking one of Tom's pieces back to the start.

> NANCY (playful, teasing)
>
> Knocked out again! Your turn, Tom.

After a few more rounds, they push the game aside.

Nancy serves the soup.

They eat in quiet companionship, the storm's howl growing louder.

Tom watches Sandra, the way she hunches over her bowl, stirring absently.

He leans forward, his voice calm, steady.

                    TOM (gentle, storytelling voice)

          Once upon a time, in a castle deep in the moun-
          tains, there lived a princess named Jasmine...

Sandra looks up, curiosity flickering through the fear in her eyes.

Nancy listens too, her lips curling into a soft smile.

But in her gaze, something deeper lingers—a longing, an ache.

                    NANCY (THOUGHTS V.O.) (soft, wistful)

          I wish I were more than just the neighbor who
          looks after his daughter.

One day, I'll tell him how I feel.

Outside, the storm howls.

Inside, they are safe.

For now.

                                        FADE OUT.

INT. TOM'S APARTMENT – KITCHEN – NIGHT

The storm has passed.

The only sound left is the occasional CREAKING of the building.

Nancy clears the table, stacking empty bowls in the sink.

At the window, Tom stands with the shutters open, peering into the darkened wreckage of the street.

DEBRIS SCATTERED.

SHADOWS STRETCHED UNDER BROKEN LAMP POSTS.

A world left behind by the storm.

Sandra appears beside him.

Her small hand reaches for his.

Tom looks down, smiles softly.

> TOM (whispering, reassuring)
> It's okay now, sweetheart.

He lifts her into his arms, carrying her back to the table.

Gently, he sets her down. Kneels before her.

> TOM (CONT'D) (hesitant, but firm)
> I have to go to work now, Sandra. Nancy will stay here and take care of you.

Sandra clings to his arm, her eyes glistening with unshed tears.

> SANDRA (whimpering, pleading)
> Do you really have to? It's so dark outside...

Nancy, holding a few worn books, watches silently.

Her hands hover over the pages before she speaks.

> NANCY (soft, warm)
> Sandra, we'll do some reading until you get sleepy. Maybe a story you like?

Sandra glances between them, her fingers tightening around Tom's sleeve.

> SANDRA (small, fragile)

Daddy, don't go.

Tom strokes her hair, his smile tender but weighed with sadness.

> TOM
>
> (gentle, but unwavering)
>
> I have to, honey. The storm must have destroyed a
> lot of things outside, and they need to be cleared a-
> way. But you're safe here, with Nancy.

Be good, okay?

Nancy nods, but concern lingers in her gaze.

> NANCY (soft, hesitant)
>
> Take care of yourself, Tom.

Tom stands, kisses Sandra's forehead, then glances at Nancy.

A brief, unspoken moment.

> TOM (low, firm)
>
> I'll be back soon.

He pulls on his jacket, casts one last look at them, then steps through the door.

The lock clicks into place behind him.

Nancy turns to Sandra, opens a book, and begins to read.

Sandra leans against her, tiny fingers gripping the pages.

The storm outside may be gone, but the real storm is just beginning.

FADE OUT.

EXT. STREET – NIGHT

Tom pushes open the front door and steps onto the sidewalk.

A few streetlights still flicker, casting weak, unreliable light over the destruction left behind by the storm.

DEBRIS IS EVERYWHERE.

Across the street, half the roof of a house is gone. A pile of rubble and shattered bricks blocks the entrance of MR. FOO'S SHOP.

In the faint glow of a streetlamp, Tom spots Foo, clearing away the wreckage, his movements slow, tired.

Tom strides across the street.

> TOM (calling out, steady)
>
> Foo! Need a hand?

Foo pauses, wipes sweat from his brow, and lets out a heavy sigh.

> FOO   (gruff, grateful)
>
> If you're offering, I won't stop you.

Together, they begin moving the heavy debris, piece by piece.

A quiet rhythm develops—the scrape of stone against pavement, the occasional grunt of effort.

When the entrance is finally cleared, Foo exhales, stretching his back.

He glances at Tom, offering a small, appreciative nod.

> FOO (CONT'D) (quiet, sincere)
>
> You can always run a tab with me, Tom. Anytime.

Foo unlocks the door, steps inside, and flips on the dim, flickering lights. A few moments later, he returns with a broom, beginning the long process of sweeping away the dust and debris.

The street slowly stirs back to life.

OTHER RESIDENTS emerge from their homes, cautiously, warily.

A sense of routine in the aftermath of destruction.

Then—

A CAR ROUNDS THE CORNER.

A low, sleek machine—one of the few still running in this city.

It pulls up beside them, the engine purring.

Tom doesn't need to look twice.

PAUL KLANCY sits in the back seat, his gaze cold, amused, assessing.

The doors swing open.

Klancy steps out, followed by two of his men. They smirk, exchanging knowing glances.

> KLANCY (mock-friendly, dangerous)
>
> Foo, my friend. Let's talk.

Foo stiffens.

Klancy places a hand on his shoulder, guiding him toward the shop with an air of casual authority.

Tom takes a step forward—

But the two men move quickly, blocking his path.

One of them, broad-shouldered and grinning, folds his arms.

MAN 1 (mocking, firm)

Don't make it harder, Tom. Stay where you are.

Tom clenches his fists, his jaw tightening.

He knows exactly what's happening.

He knows he can't stop it.

His gaze flickers toward the shop as Foo disappears inside, Klancy close behind.

Frustrated, Tom turns away.

His hands move mechanically as he lifts another piece of debris, shoving it into a pile—

But his eyes never stop darting back to the shop.

FADE OUT.

INT. FOO'S SHOP – NIGHT

The dim lighting makes the space feel even smaller.

Shelves line the walls, stocked with whatever goods Foo has managed to keep.

But the air—thick, suffocating—tastes like fear.

MR. FOO stands behind the counter, his hands shaking slightly.

PAUL KLANCY stands opposite him, arms casually crossed, a predator's grin on his face.

KLANCY (mocking, slow)

So, Foo... it's Thursday. And when was payday?

Foo swallows. His knuckles whiten as he grips the counter's edge.

His voice, when it comes, is barely a whisper.

> FOO (weak, terrified)
>
> Tuesday.

Klancy's grin disappears instantly.

A LOUD SLAM.

Klancy's palm strikes the counter, shaking the old wooden surface.

Foo flinches.

> KLANCY (dangerous, simmering rage)
>
> Exactly. Tuesday. And what do you think happens when you're late again?

Foo lowers his gaze, too afraid to answer.

> FOO (whispering, desperate)
>
> It won't happen again...

A cold chuckle escapes Klancy's lips.

Then—a swift, brutal kick.

BAM.

Klancy's boot connects with the counter, knocking over an entire row of products.

Bottles, cans, and boxes crash to the floor.

Foo jumps at the sound, but he doesn't move.

> KLANCY (quiet, venomous)
>
> It better not, Foo. Or this is just the beginning.

Foo nods frantically, words spilling over themselves.

FOO   (pleading, panicked)

I promise, I'll pay on time... I'll... I'll figure it out.

Klancy leans in, his voice dropping to a low, venomous whisper.

KLANCY (mocking, cold)

I don't care how you do it, old man. Sell more to those starving fools outside. Or find someone else to foot the bill.

ANOTHER KICK.

A display stand topples over, scattering goods everywhere.

Foo remains frozen, his breathing shallow.

Klancy doesn't even look back.

He strides toward the door, pulls it open, and steps out into the night.

The silence that follows is suffocating.

Only the faint creak of the shop door in the wind remains.

FADE OUT.

EXT. FOO'S SHOP – NIGHT

The shop door creaks open, and PAUL KLANCY emerges.

His men follow close behind, their laughter low, cruel.

Klancy spots Tom, still standing near the debris pile.

But mockery isn't enough.

He stops. Turns. Fixes his gaze on Tom.

> KLANCY (mocking, slow)
>
> Mind your own business, Tom. We know each other, right?

His smile turns wicked.

> KLANCY (CONT'D) (lower, amused)
>
> Your days of calling the shots as a cop? Long gone.

Tom doesn't react.

His fists clench, his jaw tightens—but he doesn't move.

Klancy watches him for a beat, satisfied, before turning to his men.

> KLANCY (CONT'D) (bored, dismissive)
>
> Let's go. We've got bigger things to handle.

The men chuckle, exchange glances, then climb back into the car.

Klancy settles into the back seat, and the engine rumbles to life.

With a roar, the car peels away, disappearing into the darkened city streets.

FOO steps out of the shop, standing beside Tom.

His rage is barely contained.

His eyes glow with frustration, helplessness.

> FOO (low, angry)
>
> Damn storm. Damn Paul Klancy. When does this end?

Tom watches the car's taillights fade, his own thoughts a storm within him.

He places a firm hand on Foo's shoulder.

> TOM (quiet, steady)
>
> Take care, Foo.

Then, he turns, crosses the street, and walks home.

Under the dim glow of the streetlights, he looks like a man trapped in a war he can't win.

> FADE OUT.

INT. TOM'S APARTMENT – NIGHT

Tom pushes open the apartment door.

The storm outside is gone, but inside, the air still feels heavy.

At the kitchen table, NANCY and SANDRA tidy up school supplies.

Sandra, her movements slow with exhaustion, carefully packs her things into a small backpack.

She wanders to the sink, standing on her tiptoes, trying to reach the faucet as she brushes her teeth.

Tom leans against the wall, his gaze shifting to Nancy. His voice is low, measured.

> TOM (quiet, tense)
>
> Paul Klancy was here. He put the squeeze on
> Foo again. Half the street saw it, and no one did
> a damn thing.

Nancy stiffens, her brow furrowed in deep concern.

> NANCY (shaking her head, voice tight)

That man… I don't know how Foo survives this.

Tom exhales sharply, casting a glance at Sandra, still brushing her teeth. He pushes off the wall, walking toward the door.

TOM   (soft, but firm)

Thanks for looking after Sandra today. You remember I have to work early tomorrow? Can you come again?

Nancy's lips curl into a small, knowing smile.

NANCY (gentle, warm)

Of course. I wouldn't forget something like that.

Tom meets her eyes—briefly, but intensely.

TOM (low, sincere)

I know you're not doing this for the little gold I can give you. Thank you.

Nancy chuckles softly, slipping on her jacket.

NANCY (half-joking, but honest)

It's no trouble, Tom. Really, it's not.

Tom closes the door behind her, hesitating for a moment, his hand lingering on the bolt.

Then, he turns away, heading for the living room.

Sandra lies curled up on the couch, a blanket draped over her, a small stuffed animal clutched in her arms.

Tom kneels beside her, tucking the blanket closer, before pressing a soft kiss to her forehead.

TOM (whispering, tender)

Good night, sweetheart.

Sandra murmurs sleepily, her words lost in drowsiness.

Tom blows out the candle on the table and steps away, leaving the door slightly ajar, allowing the warm glow from the kitchen candle to spill into the room.

INT. TOM'S APARTMENT – KITCHEN – NIGHT

Tom moves with slow, deliberate motions, opening a cupboard.

He pulls out a small metal tin and a kitchen scale.

With careful precision, he pours the contents of the tin onto the scale—small gold pieces, painstakingly earned from countless jobs.

He stares at the weight.

His expression darkens.

                    TOM (muttering, to himself)
          It's not enough...

His jaw tightens. Frustrated, he scoops the gold back into the tin, shutting it away.

He reaches for another cupboard, retrieving a bottle of gin and a glass.

Sitting at the kitchen table, the candlelight flickering, he pours himself a drink.

Hc takes a slow sip, starlng blankly at the glass.

The silence is thick, suffocating.

Then—a flood of memories crashes in.

                                        FADE TO FLASH-
                                        BACK.

EXT. STREET – NIGHT (FLASHBACK)

The city is quiet. Streetlights cast a soft glow on the pavement.

TOM and TANJA walk arm in arm, their laughter gentle in the silence.

Their steps light, carefree—a moment of normalcy.

A car approaches from the opposite direction. Its headlights flare, illuminating their path.

> TANJA (laughing, teasing)
>
> Did you see the waiter's face when you told him it was the best wine?

Tom chuckles, shaking his head.

> TOM (grinning)
>
> He didn't even know what he was serving!

The car slows as it passes.

Then—GUNSHOTS.

The world shatters.

Tom and Tanja collapse.

Tanja's scream cuts short.

The car tires screech, vanishing into the darkness.

Tom lies on the cold pavement, his hand clutching his side—blood seeping through his fingers.

Groaning, he turns his head—

Tanja lies motionless nearby.

> TOM (CONT'D) (strangled, desperate)

Tanja… no…!

With trembling arms, he crawls toward her, gathering her limp body in his arms.

Her eyes are half-open, her breath shallow.

> TANJA (weak, fading)
>
> Tom…

Her voice barely a whisper.

Tom holds her tighter, his hands shaking.

> TOM   (choked, pleading)
>
> Stay with me. Please, Tanja. Don't…

Tanja tries to smile, but her strength is gone.

Her eyes slowly close.

A final shudder runs through her body—and then, stillness.

Tom clutches her, his face contorted in silent agony.

As the car disappears, he catches a glimpse of the shooter's face in the rear window.

A grinning silhouette, burning itself into his memory.

Tom's expression changes.

Pain twists into anger.

The camera lingers on his broken but determined face, blood dripping onto the pavement.

> FADE OUT.

<u>END FLASHBACK.</u>

INT. TOM'S APARTMENT – KITCHEN – NIGHT

Tom jerks back to the present.

His breathing is heavy, his hands trembling around the glass.

The candle flickers, casting long shadows across his face.

He reaches for the bottle of gin, pouring another measure into the glass.

Lifting it to his lips, he pauses—staring at his reflection in the liquid.

His own voice, barely a whisper.

TOM (low, bitter)
You have to stay strong.

He leans back, letting the burn of alcohol settle in his throat.

And then, like a tide, his thoughts pull him back again.

FADE TO FLASH-
BACK.

EXT. DARK ALLEY – NIGHT (FLASHBACK)

A narrow alley, lit only by moonlight and dim streetlamps.

TOM, in uniform, a gun drawn, sprints down the passage.

Ahead, a man flees, slipping into shadows.

Tom's breath is ragged, but he won't stop now.

TOM (yelling, commanding)

Stop! Police!

The man doesn't listen—he runs faster.

Tom grits his teeth, holsters his gun, and pushes forward.

At the alley's end—he catches up.

With a powerful lunge, Tom tackles the man down.

They roll, struggling, fists flying.

Then—a glint of movement.

The man's hand lunges for Tom's holster.

A SHOT RINGS OUT.

Silence.

Tom stares down at the man—motionless, a bullet wound in his chest.

And then—he recognizes the face.

The man who killed his wife.

Tom's grip on the gun tightens.

A moment of relief—

But mostly, emptiness.

FADE OUT.

INT. POLICE STATION – DAY

Tom stands stiffly in front of Captain Miller's desk.

On the wooden surface, his badge and service weapon lie still, symbols of a life he is leaving behind.

His movements are deliberate, heavy as he sets them down for the last time.

Miller watches him, his expression tight with conflict. He wants to say something, but the words die in his throat.

After a long pause, he simply nods.

> MILLER (soft, hesitant)
>
> Tom… I know how hard this must have been…

Tom lifts a hand, stopping him before he can continue.

His gaze never lifts from the desk. His voice is steady, but hollow.

> TOM (quiet, final)
>
> I'm done, Miller.

Miller looks away.

The silence is suffocating.

Tom turns, hesitates for the briefest of moments, then walks out.

His footsteps echo through the long, empty hallway as he leaves the station forever.

FADE OUT.

INT. TOM'S APARTMENT – KITCHEN – MORNING

The first rays of sunlight filter through the cracks in the steel shutters, painting the kitchen in streaks of light and shadow.

Tom unlatches the shutters, swinging them open. The fresh morning air seeps in.

Across the small room, Sandra stirs, stretching before padding off to the bathroom.

The faint sound of running water follows—Sandra's morning routine.

Tom turns to the stove, pouring fresh coffee grounds into boiling water. The aroma fills the space, blending with the faint sounds of the waking city.

Sandra returns, her hands quickly making sandwiches, her small fingers deft and practiced.

Tom leans against the counter, watching her for a moment.

> TOM   (casual, but warm)
>
> The weather looks good today. Maybe you and
> Nancy can go out, do something fun.

Sandra nods, her expression lightening.

She places the sandwiches on a plate and carries them to the table.

> SANDRA (half-smiling, teasing)
>
> Maybe we'll go to the park… but only if the stupid storm doesn't come
> back.

Tom chuckles, shaking his head as he joins her at the table.

They eat in comfortable silence, the moment familiar, peaceful.

As Tom finishes his coffee, he stands, setting his mug in the sink.

Reaching for his jacket, he pulls it on.

Sandra watches him—her eyes carrying a quiet sadness, though she keeps it to herself.

SANDRA (CONT'D) (soft, determined)

Daddy, I'll be good. I promise.

Tom kneels in front of her, his smile gentle.

He presses a soft kiss to her forehead.

TOM (tender, reassuring)

I know, sweetheart. Be good and have fun with
Nancy, okay?

Sandra nods, her smile small but genuine.

Tom squeezes her shoulder, then heads for the door.

INT. HALLWAY – MORNING

Tom walks down the hallway, stopping in front of Nancy's door.

He knocks lightly.

A moment later, the door creaks open, revealing Nancy—her expression warm as
always.

TOM (quiet, appreciative)

Thanks for watching Sandra.

Nancy smiles, nodding without hesitation.

NANCY   (gentle, reassuring)

You know I'm happy to do it. She'll be just fine with
me.

Tom exhales slightly, his shoulders loosening just a bit.

TOM (soft, sincere)

I know. Thanks, Nancy.

They share a brief look, a moment of understanding unspoken.

Then Tom turns, heading for the stairs.

Nancy watches him leave, her expression lingering before she quietly closes the door.

FADE OUT.

EXT. STREET – DAY

Tom walks slowly down the ruined street.

The storm's aftermath is everywhere—shattered windows, broken rooftops, debris-strewn sidewalks.

A few residents work silently, piling wreckage into makeshift heaps.

In the middle of the street, a Red Cross van idles.

Workers, masked and gloved, move mechanically.

They lift bodies, one by one, placing them gently into the back of the van.

No one speaks.

The air is thick, the only sounds—crunching debris under boots, the dull clang of metal.

Tom pauses, watching.

His face is still, but his eyes flicker—a brief hint of unease, of sorrow.

A worker pulls the doors shut with a muted thud.

The sound lingers, bouncing off the hollow streets.

The van's engine rumbles to life, rolling forward, the Red Cross emblem fading into the distance.

Tom turns his head slightly, watching until it disappears around a corner.

His expression doesn't change—but something in his eyes does.

FADE OUT.

EXT. GATHERING POINT – DAY

A dusty expanse, littered with debris, filled with restless men—young and old, desperate.

Tom steps into the chaos, eyes scanning the crowd.

Around him, the shouting begins.

TRUCKS pull in, engines growling, foremen shouting orders.

The men push forward, calling out.

> LABORER 1 (desperate, loud)
>
> I can lift anything! Take me!

> LABORER 2 (pleading, frantic)
>
> I'll work for half the pay!

Tom raises his voice, stepping forward.

> TOM (strong, assertive)
>
> I've got experience! I can help!

But the crowd is too thick, the voices too many.

A man shoves past him, scrambling for attention.

Time ticks away—men either get work or leave, disappointed.

The noise fades, trucks pulling out, leaving only a handful of stragglers.

Tom wipes the sweat from his forehead, leaning against a truck.

A foreman steps out, clipboard in hand.

Their eyes meet—recognition flickers.

The foreman nods once.

> FOREMAN   (gruff, but familiar)
>
> Still looking, Tom?

Tom shrugs slightly.

> TOM (dry, tired)
>
> Like everyone else.

The foreman studies him, then gestures at the clipboard.

> FOREMAN (business-like, firm)
>
> I've got something. Night shift. Security work. You in?

Tom hesitates. Just for a moment.

Then he nods.

His voice is low, steady—but with a hint of relief.

> TOM
>
> Yeah. Sure. Thanks.

The foreman scribbles something, hands Tom a small slip of paper.

> FOREMAN

Be on time. You know how it works.

Tom takes the paper, folding it into his pocket.

He casts one last glance at the emptying lot, then turns away.

He walks off—another job, another night.

FADE OUT.

EXT. HARBOR KIOSK – DAY

The sun hangs low in the sky, casting a pale, cold light over the HARBOR. At a small KI-OSK near the docks, Tom stands with the CAPTAIN of the African Star. The captain, a weathered man with sharp eyes, holds a steaming CUP OF COFFEE in his hand. Both lean casually against the kiosk counter, though the tension on Tom's face betrays the gravity of their conversation.

TOM (thoughtfully)

When does the ship leave?

The captain sips his coffee, his gaze sweeping over the harbor before answering.

CAPTAIN (calmly, firmly)

Tomorrow. The storms are getting worse, and there won't be another ship coming. Not for months.

The words hang heavily in the air. Tom stares into his COFFEE CUP, his brow furrowed. It's too little time. His expression reveals both concern and determination.

TOM (hesitant, urgent)

That's tight... way too tight. But waiting another year?

The captain remains composed, taking another sip of his coffee and waiting for Tom to continue.

TOM (CONT'D) (cautiously, pleading)

170

Can we work something out on the price? I can work
on board—whatever you need. I'll do anything.

The captain shakes his head slowly, placing his cup back down.

                    CAPTAI (firmly)

The price is fixed. There's nothing I can do, not even
for you.

He looks at Tom with a mix of sympathy and hard reality.

                    CAPTAIN (CONT'D) (serious, almost bitter)

I'll hold the spots for you, Wagner. But without payment? No

way. You have to understand, I lost my sympathy for
this kind of thing a long time ago.

He pats Tom on the shoulder in a gesture of encouragement, his tone softening
slightly.

                    CAPTAIN (CONT'D) (encouragingly)

I'm counting on you.

The captain tosses his empty cup into a nearby trash can and walks away, heading toward his ship with measured steps. Tom stays behind, watching him leave, the weight
of his worries clear on his face.

He takes the last sip of his coffee, throws the cup into the trash, and turns away. With a
determined look, he walks slowly down the street, his mind racing.

                                        FADE OUT.

EXT. TOM'S STREET – DAY

Tom (tense, alert) turns onto his street and suddenly stops.

Something feels off.

A CROWD has gathered in front of Mr. Foo's shop.

Two POLICE CARS are parked diagonally across the street, their lights flashing silently—no sirens, just the cold finality of a crime.

Tom (focused, uneasy) takes a deep breath, his gaze sharpening.

He quickens his steps, moving with purpose through the crowd. The voices around him are muffled, anxious, full of tension.

An older neighbor (worried, shaken), his face lined with exhaustion, notices Tom approaching and steps closer.

NEIGHBOR (LOWERING HIS VOICE, CAUTIOUS, FEARFUL)

Tom... have you heard? Foo... they shot him. Right in front of his shop.

Tom (shocked but controlled, anger simmering beneath the surface) looks toward the shop, where a group of POLICE OFFICERS is setting up crime scene tape.

The neighbor (nervous, glancing around before whispering) leans in, covering his mouth with his hand.

NEIGHBOR (HESITANT, AFRAID)

I saw it. Klancy's car. He sped off, tires screeching.

Tom's jaw tightens, his fists clenching slightly, but he says nothing.

His eyes scan the scene, stopping when he spots a POLICE OFFICER writing in a notebook near one of the cars.

Recognition flickers across Tom's face.

TOM (LOW, FIRM, FILLED WITH HISTORY)

Paul Masters.

He walks toward him.

Masters, a middle-aged cop (exhausted but decent, wary), looks up and offers a tired but genuine smile.

MASTERS (SOFT CHUCKLE, WEARY WARMTH)

Tom Wagner. It's been a while.

They shake hands, but the moment is heavy with unspoken words.

Masters (serious, lowering his voice, glancing at the other officers) leans in slightly.

MASTERS (QUIET, FIRM, REGRETFUL)

Foo's dead, Tom. Two shots to the chest. Right in front of his shop.

Tom (composed but burning inside, voice steady but tight) nods.

TOM (CONTROLLED, POINTED, EXPECTING THE TRUTH)

Do you know who did it?

Masters (sighs, conflicted, scanning the area nervously) hesitates before stepping even closer.

MASTERS (LOW, RESIGNED, FRUSTRATED)

We all know. But nothing's going to happen. Klancy's got his hooks in deep here... You know how it is. Anyone who won't take his bribes has their family to worry about.

Tom (staring, jaw clenched, a storm brewing in his eyes) doesn't respond immediately.

Masters (genuine, regretful, cautious) places a brief but firm hand on Tom's shoulder.

MASTERS (SINCERE, WARNING TONE) (CONT'D)

Take care of yourself, Tom.

They exchange a brief, knowing nod before Masters steps back, gets into the police car, and pulls away.

The police vehicles disappear, their flashing lights fading into the distance.

Tom (rigid, standing still, lost in thought) watches them go.

Then, without a word, he turns and enters his HOUSE, his movements calm but his eyes filled with silent rage.

FADE OUT.

INT. TOM'S APARTMENT – DAY

Tom (tense, deep in thought, carrying the weight of the news) opens the door and steps inside.

The room is quiet, but the air is thick with unspoken tension.

Nancy (worried, protective, maternal) sits on the COUCH, with Sandra (distressed, vulnerable, shaken) beside her, clinging tightly.

Sandra's face is streaked with tears, her small body trembling slightly.

Nancy (soft, comforting, warm) speaks gently, her tone soothing and steady.

NANCY (CALM, REASSURING)

It's okay, Sandra. You're safe here. Daddy's home now.

Tom (softens immediately, concerned, fatherly instinct kicking in) kneels in front of Sandra and gently takes her in his arms.

TOM (SOOTHING, STEADY, PROTECTIVE)

Hey, sweetheart. Everything's going to be alright. You know what? I just got a new job for tonight. And soon, I'll have enough saved up so we can all leave this place together.

Sandra (sniffles, hopeful but hesitant, clinging to him) wipes her tears and looks up at him with wide eyes.

SANDRA (INNOCENT, HOPEFUL, LOOKING FOR REASSURANCE)

Will Nancy come with us too?

Tom (surprised by the question, exchanging a look with Nancy, a moment of something deeper passing between them) glances at her.

Nancy (caught off guard, touched, her heart tightening slightly) meets his gaze, then smiles softly.

They both know how uncertain the future is.

Nancy (quickly regaining composure, lighthearted, trying to lift the mood) jumps in, her tone playful but sincere.

> NANCY (GRINNING, TEASING, AF-
> FECTIONATE)
>
> Of course, I will. I can't leave you alone. Who else
> would make sure you don't get into trouble?

Sandra (relieved, smiling through her tears, finally calming down) nods.

Tom (grateful, warm, a rare softness in his voice) looks at Nancy, his expression filled with appreciation.

> TOM (GENUINE, EARNEST, A QUIET MOMENT OF
> HONESTY)
>
> Thank you, Nancy. Really. And... I'm sorry for al-
> ways asking you to help. I know you've done so
> much for us. But I don't have a choice. I have to
> take every job I can.

Nancy (shaking her head, brushing it off but touched by his words) waves her hand dismissively and smiles warmly.

> NANCY (REASSURING, CARING, AF-
> FECTIONATE)
>
> Don't worry about it, Tom. You and Sandra mean a
> lot to me. I'm happy to help.

Tom (standing, placing a protective hand on Sandra's shoulder, shifting the mood) glances between Sandra and Nancy.

> TOM (LIGHTER, SHIFTING GEARS, FATHERLY
> ENERGY RETURNING)

How about we all go to the park for a bit? Some fresh
air would do us good.

Sandra (excited, mood lifting, her energy returning) nods eagerly.

> SANDRA (ENTHUSIASTIC, JOYFUL, FULL OF
> CHILDLIKE EXCITEMENT)

Yes, please, Daddy!

Nancy (smiling, warm, looking at them both with fondness, reaching for her jacket)
nods.

> NANCY (CHEERFUL, ENCOURAGING, TEASING
> SLIGHTLY)

Let's go then, before we change our minds.

The three of them gather their things and head for the door.

The tense weight of the earlier events begins to fade, replaced by a subtle, fragile hope.

As they step outside, the door clicks shut behind them, marking a moment of
escape—however temporary it may be.

FADE OUT.

EXT. PARK – DAY

The SUN shines brightly, a rare day without storms. The PARK is bustling, filled with
laughter and chatter. On an OLD PLAYGROUND, children climb on the JUNGLE
GYM, while on a grassy FIELD surrounded by piles of debris, boys play soccer with
carefree joy. For a moment, the world seems normal again.

SANDRA swings happily on her FAVORITE SWING, her face glowing with delight as
she pumps her legs to go higher. Nearby, TOM and NANCY relax on a PICNIC BLAN-
KET. Tom lies back with his hands behind his head, while Nancy sits upright, hugging
her knees. They speak softly.

> NANCY (SOFT, REFLECTIVE, VOICE
> TREMBLING SLIGHTLY)

You know, I used to have everything... a family, a

home. But then... the storm came. The first big one.
We didn't stand a chance.

Tom opens his eyes, looking at her. Her gaze is distant, her voice trembling slightly.

NANCY (SWALLOWING HARD, STRUGGLING

WITH THE WORDS) (CONT'D)

My husband... my parents... all gone. Since then...
piece by piece, I lost everything that mattered to
me.

She pauses, turns to Tom, her eyes filled with gratitude—and something more.

NANCY (SOFTER, A HINT OF WARMTH

RETURNING) (CONT'D)

Until I found refuge with you and Sandra.

She smiles softly, her cheeks flushing slightly.

NANCY (GENTLE, HONEST, EMOTIONAL) (CONT'D)

You're the only thing that's given me a little hope
again.

Tom looks at her, moved by her words. A moment of silence passes, broken only
by the distant laughter of children.

Tom reaches out and takes Nancy's HAND, holding it gently as he gazes into her eyes.

The mood shifts, growing more intense. They lean slightly toward each other, as if
about to share a kiss...

SUDDENLY, SANDRA bursts in, laughing and brimming with excitement.

SANDRA (CHEERFUL, COMPLETELY UNAWARE
OF THE MOMENT SHE JUST INTERRUPTED)

Daddy, come on! Let's ride the merry-go-
round!

Tom laughs, releasing Nancy's hand as he gets to his feet.

TOM (TEASING, WARM, FULL OF LOVE FOR HIS DAUGHTER)

Alright, alright! But only if I can keep up!

He runs off with Sandra toward the PLAYGROUND. Nancy remains seated on the blanket, watching them with a smile. A single TEAR rolls down her cheek as she takes in the scene, feeling a bittersweet mix of joy and longing.

FADE OUT.

EXT. DAY LABORERS' GATHERING PLACE – NIGHT

The area is cloaked in DARKNESS, dimly lit by flickering streetlights. Despite the late hour, the DAY LABORERS' GATHERING PLACE is alive with frantic activity. Men of all ages crowd together, shouting and gesturing wildly. The air is thick with desperation.

Tom approaches the area, his posture steady, but his face betrays a mix of weariness and determination. By a PICKUP TRUCK, the FOREMAN—a burly man with a weathered face—stands with a CLIPBOARD, jotting down the names of the lucky few selected for work.

Tom pushes his way through the shouting crowd, ignoring the frantic calls around him. The noise is chaotic and tinged with anger.

MAN 1 (desperate, shouting)

Take me! I can work all night!

MAN 2 (pleading, voice cracking)

I'll do it for half the pay!

Tom presses forward, his jaw set, as he shoulders past a younger man, who shoots him an angry glare.

YOUNG MAN (grumbling, bitterly)

Watch it, old man.

Tom doesnâ€Ô t react, his eyes fixed on the foreman. When the foreman spots him, a flicker of recognition and relief crosses his face.

FOREMAN (loud, gruff)

Wagner! Over here.

Tom steps forward, and the foreman scribbles his name onto the clipboard. His voice softens slightly, carrying a hint of respect.

FOREMAN (CONT'D) (matter-of-fact, curt)

Get on. You're in.

Tom climbs onto the TRUCK'S FLATBED. Several other men are already seated, their faces drawn and tired, their clothes worn. No one speaks. Brief glances are exchanged before their eyes drop to the floor.

The foreman slams the FLATBED GATE shut with a loud clang. He casts a final look at the crowd, then climbs into the cab and starts the engine.

The PICKUP rumbles to life, the roar of the motor drowning out the desperate shouts from the remaining men.

MAN 3 (yelling, with a final glimmer of hope)

Wait! Take me too!

The camera lingers on the crowd as it begins to disperse, some men leaving in resignation, others arguing angrily among themselves. Finally, it shifts to Tom on the flatbed. His gaze is fixed ahead, distant, as the wind brushes through his hair.

The other men sit silently, their breaths visible in the cold night air. The weight of their situation hangs over them like an unspoken shadow.

FADE OUT.

EXT. PLANTATION FENCES – NIGHT

A dusty JEEP rumbles along the outer fences of a vast PLANTATION. The night sky is dark, stars obscured by patches of clouds. A strong WIND rustles the tall grass, adding to the eerie atmosphere.

TOM sits in the passenger seat, operating a powerful SPOTLIGHT that sweeps across the fences and fields. ROB (50), a crazed ex-soldier with a restless demeanor and a penchant for ridiculous stories, drives with an infectious, almost inappropriate laugh.

ROB   (loud, animated)

And then the idiot throws the wrong grenade! Hah!
Picture this, Tom. We're all flat on the ground, and
he... boom! Smoke grenade, right in the middle of the
fight!

Tom shoots him an annoyed glance but says nothing, his focus fixed on the spotlight
scanning the fence line.

TOM (dryly)

Riveting, Rob. Really.

Rob grins, unfazed by Tom's lack of enthusiasm.

ROB (with exaggerated enthusiasm)

Oh, come on! You gotta laugh a little. These nights
are boring as hell without some humor.

Suddenly, the spotlight catches something unusual—a HOLE in the FENCE. Tom's
expression hardens.

TOM (calmly, tense)

Rob, stop the car.

Rob slams on the brakes. The Jeep screeches to a halt. Both men climb out, their
boots crunching on the dry ground. Tom directs his flashlight at the hole, while Rob
leans in for a closer look.

ROB (skeptical, low voice)

Looks fresh. Whoever did this isn't far.

Tom nods, his eyes tracing faint TRACKS in the dirt. He heads back to the Jeep and retrieves a RIFLE and two HANDHELD SPOTLIGHTS. He hands one to Rob.

TOM (resolutely)

Let's follow it.

Rob takes the spotlight, checking its battery before flicking it on. His grin fades, replaced
by a more serious demeanor.

ROB (grumbling, almost annoyed)

Alright, let's play hero then.

The two men follow the TRACKS, their spotlights cutting through the dark. The wind picks up, the night grows darker, and every step carries a palpable tension.

FADE OUT.

EXT. FIELD – NIGHT

The spotlights cut through the darkness as Tom and Rob push through the tall GRASS. The night is eerily quiet, except for the rustling of the WIND. Suddenly, the beam lands on a GROUP OF CHILDREN crouched in the field, stuffing POTATOES into SACKS.

The children freeze, terror etched on their faces. They drop to the ground, trembling under the glare of the lights.

ROB (loud, aggressive)

You little bastards! Hands off! Now!

Rob pulls a set of ZIP TIES from his pocket, his movements sharp and menacing.

TOM   (firmly, pleading)

Rob, wait! They're just kids. They're hungry.
Let them go.

Rob stops, his eyes burning with anger as he turns to Tom.

ROB (angry, mocking)

Hungry? So what? That doesn't give them the right
to steal. Rules are rules.

TOM (calm but stern)

These aren't criminals, Rob. They're desperate.

Rob tosses the zip ties to the ground and takes a step closer to Tom, his face contorted with rage.

> ROB (hissing, dangerously calm)

I've had enough of your bleeding-heart crap.

Suddenly, Rob grabs Tom and wrenches the RIFLE out of his hands. With practiced precision, he aims it at Tom.

> ROB (CONT'D) (menacing)

Now you're going to do what I say. Tie them up.
Now.

Tom hesitates, his hands trembling slightly, but Rob raises the rifle higher, his finger hovering near the trigger.

> TOM (desperate)

This is wrong, Rob. Stop this.

> ROB (coldly)

Tie. Them. Up.

Reluctantly, Tom kneels and begins to tie the children's hands with the zip ties. The children cry softly, their faces pale with fear. Rob gestures sharply.

> ROB (CONT'D) (yelling)

Move it! To the truck.

EXT. PICKUP TRUCK – NIGHT

At the truck, Rob forces Tom to lift the children onto the flatbed. Tom's face is filled with anguish as he carefully helps the trembling children into the truck.

> ROB (snarling)

Faster, Wagner. We don't have time for your pity
party.

Once the children are loaded, Rob orders Tom into the driver's seat. Rob climbs into the passenger seat, the RIFLE pointed steadily at Tom.

INT. PICKUP TRUCK – NIGHT

Tom starts the engine, his hands trembling on the steering wheel. As they drive off, he glances at Rob, his voice calm but imploring.

> TOM (pleading, soft)
>
> Rob, please. Think about this. These are kids. They don't deserve this. They need help.

> ROB (coldly, without looking at him)
>
> Shut up, Wagner. You're too soft. That's your problem.

Tom persists, his tone growing firmer but still controlled.

> TOM (intensely)
>
> You know this is wrong. Stop now, before it's too late.

> ROB (shouting, with a bitter laugh)
>
> Too late? It was too late the moment these little thieves decided to break the rules!

The camera lingers on Tom, his face a mixture of anger and helplessness, as the truck rumbles through the dark night.

FADE OUT.

EXT. PLANTATION COMPOUND – NIGHT

The PICKUP rolls into the dusty COMPOUND, its tires crunching loudly over gravel. The TRUCK'S HEADLIGHTS cast long, eerie shadows on the ADMINISTRATION BUILDING, which looms ominously in the dark. Rob sits in the passenger seat, the RIFLE still aimed steadily at Tom, who grips the wheel tightly, his face tense.

The truck comes to a stop, and Rob immediately gets out, his movements sharp and commanding.

Tom slowly opens the driver's door, glancing back at the truck bed, where the terrified CHILDREN huddle together.

Rob calls over a group of WORKERS who have been standing idly nearby, drawn by the noise of the truck.

                    ROB (loud, authoritative)

        Hey, you! Get over here! Take the kids off the truck
        and lock them in the storage room.

The workers exchange brief glances but obey without question. They approach the truck, pulling the children down one by one and leading them away. The children whimper softly, their wide eyes filled with fear.

                    TOM (firmly, desperate)

        Rob, stop this. They're just kids. You know this is
        wrong.

Rob turns slowly to Tom, his eyes cold and unrelenting.

                    ROB (hissing)

        Shut up, Wagner. You're not here to make decisions.

Rob pulls out a RADIO from his pocket and speaks into it.

                    ROB (CONT'D)

                (matter-of-fact, emotion-
                  less)

        This is Rob at the plantation. Got work for you. Get
        here now.

He stows the radio away and turns back to Tom. With a sharp motion, he raises the rifle, gesturing toward the administration building.

                    ROB (CONT'D) (forced calm, threatening)

        Move, Wagner. The boss wants to see you.

Tom hesitates, his face a mixture of defiance and anger. Rob jabs him lightly in the back with the rifle.

                    TOM   (low, seething)

        You're making a huge mistake.

ROB (mocking grin)

I'm just doing my job.

Reluctantly, Tom starts toward the administration building, his shoulders stiff. The camera lingers on the workers as they lead the children to a small, windowless STO-RAGE ROOM. The heavy METAL DOOR slams shut with a dull thud. Muffled cries and whimpers echo briefly before fading into silence.

Rob follows Tom, the rifle never wavering as he drives him into the building. The camera tracks their figures as they disappear into the shadows.

FADE OUT.

INT. FOREMAN'S OFFICE – NIGHT

The OFFICE is sparse, the air thick with the smell of tobacco and cheap coffee. FO-REMAN SMITH, a heavyset man in his late 40s with a sweat-slicked face, sits behind a battered wooden desk. A full ashtray and half-empty glass of whiskey sit in front of him. Rob stands with his arms crossed, the rifle slung lazily over his shoulder. Tom stands nearby, tense, his hands clenched into fists.

ROB (arrogant, loud)

So there they were, little thieves right out
in the field with sacks full of potatoes.
And our hero here... (points mockingly
at Tom) ...wanted to let them go. Can
you believe that, Smith?

Smith glares at Tom with disdain before pushing
back his chair with a loud creak. He leans heavily
on the desk, his angry eyes boring into Tom.

SMITH (yelling, furious)

What the hell were you thinking, Wagner? Those kids
could've cleaned out half the field, and you wanted to
let them go? Are you out of your damn mind?

Tom struggles to keep his composure, but his voice quivers slightly with restrained anger.

TOM (firmly, controlled)

They're just kids. They were

hungry. They took a few potatoes, not enough to
justify this.

Smith slams a fist on the desk, his face turning red.

SMITH (angrily, mockingly)

Hungry? And what about my losses? What about
the damn rules? You're here to do the job, not to tell
me what's right or wrong!

Smith pulls an envelope from a drawer and slams it onto the desk. He shoves it toward Tom with a sharp motion.

SMITH (CONT'D) (cold, scornful)

Here's your pay. And you're done, Wagner. You're
lucky I'm not docking you for damages or reporting
this to the police. Get out.

Tom stares at Smith, his breathing heavy. Before he can respond, Rob bursts
out laughing, loud and derisive.

ROB (sarcastic, mocking)

Well, Wagner. Maybe you should become a teacher.
Seems like you've got a soft spot for little criminals.

Smith gestures sharply toward the door.

SMITH (cutting)

Get out. And don't ever show your face here
again.

Rob grabs the rifle, gives Tom a rough slap on the shoulder, and continues laughing.

ROB (grinning)

Come on, hero. Time to leave the premises.

Smith sinks back into his creaking chair, taking a long drink of whiskey as Tom and Rob leave the office. Tom's face is hard, his fists clenched, but he says nothing.

FADE OUT.

EXT. APARTMENT BUILDING – NIGHT

The STREET is eerily quiet, illuminated by a few flickering streetlights. The MOON casts a faint glow through heavy clouds, and the wind carries an unsettling rustle. The silence is broken by the distant rumble of ENGINES.

A CONVOY of vehicles rolls down the street, coming to a halt in front of an APART-MENT BUILDING. Their headlights cast ominous shadows on the building's facade. The engines die, and the car doors open with metallic CLANKS.

About 15 MEN emerge, armed with RIFLES, HANDGUNS, and CROWBARS. Their loud voices and raucous laughter echo through the street. Their LEADER, PAUL KLANCY, a sharply dressed man in his mid-40s with a cold, calculating smile, steps out of the first vehicle. His demeanor is calm, almost casual.

KLANCY (calmly, with icy authority)

Listen up, boys. This building... is open for business.
Make it count – let the whole neighborhood know.

The men cheer loudly, their voices overlapping in the dark night.

MAN 1 (shouting, excited)

Let's go, boys!

With raucous laughter, they charge toward the building. Klancy stays behind, leaning casually against the hood of his car as he lights a thick CIGAR. One of his MEN stands beside him, lighting his own cigar with slightly shaky hands.

KLANCY (dryly, with a hint of sarcasm)

Oh, and don't forget to look for a few new workers
for the lab. The product doesn't cook itself.

The men burst into the BUILDING, kicking the door open. Instantly, the sound of SCREAMS, CHEERS, and GUNSHOTS erupts from inside. Klancy exhales a plume of smoke, watching the chaos unfold with a faint smirk.

KLANCY (CONT'D) (quietly, almost jokingly, to his companion)

Let's hope they don't kill everyone. We really
need more hands.

His companion chuckles nervously, though his eyes betray unease. Klancy remains entirely at ease as the noise from the building grows louder. Inside, furniture is smashed, voices shout in anger, and the faint crackle of flames becomes audible.

The camera lingers on Klancy, his face illuminated by the flickering lights from the building. His smirk doesn't falter, cold and unshaken.

FADE OUT.

INT. TOM'S APARTMENT – NIGHT

The apartment is dark, lit only by the flicker of CANDLES on the table. NANCY sits beside SANDRA, who clings to her, sobbing. The SCREAMS and GUNSHOTS from the hallway echo through the thin walls, a constant reminder of the chaos outside.

Nancy tries to calm Sandra, but her own voice trembles with fear.

NANCY (whispering, shaking)

It's going to be okay, Sandra. I'm here. I won't leave
you.

Sandra sobs harder, clutching Nancy tightly.

SANDRA (crying)

I want Daddy...

The screams grow louder, accompanied by heavy THUDS. FOOTSTEPS approach the apartment door. Nancy and Sandra freeze, holding their breath.

Suddenly, the DOOR SPLINTERS open with a deafening CRASH. Three armed MEN storm in, yelling and laughing.

MAN 1 (loud, mocking)

Well, what do we have here?

Nancy screams, trying to shield Sandra behind her. The men grab them roughly, ignoring their cries.

> NANCY (screaming, desperate)

Let us go! You monsters!

> MAN 2 (laughing)

Shut up, sweetheart! You're coming with us.

They drag Nancy and Sandra out into the HALLWAY. One of the men turns back and shouts:

> MAN 3 (commanding)

Tear the place apart! Take anything worth something!

Another man nods and rushes back into the apartment.

In the hallway, PAUL KLANCY emerges from the stairwell, a cigar in hand. He surveys Nancy and Sandra with a cold smile.

> KLANCY (calm, arrogant)

Well, well. What do we have here? Fresh stock, it seems.

Nancy struggles free, standing protectively in front of Sandra. Her voice trembles with anger.

> NANCY (loud, furious)

Leave us alone, you bastard!

Klancy chuckles, unaffected by her defiance.

> KLANCY (mocking tone)

Perfect for the lab... and maybe for something else.

The men around him laugh and cheer in agreement.

Klancy leans closer, his eyes narrowing as he examines Sandra. She hides behind Nancy, her face pale with fear.

                    KLANCY (CONT'D) (thoughtfully)

          Wait a second... aren't you Wagner's little girl?
          Tom's kid?

Sandra retreats further behind Nancy, who glares at Klancy, her voice sharp.

                    NANCY (bravely, defiant)

          That's none of your business.

Klancy stares at Nancy for a moment, a cold smile spreading across his face. He raises a hand, signaling his men to stop.

                    KLANCY (calmly, commanding)

          These two get special treatment. Don't touch
          them.

The men grumble in disappointment, but Klancy quickly reignites their enthusiasm.

                    KLANCY (CONT'D) (grinning)

          Don't worry. You'll still get to torch the place
                              when we're done.

The men cheer and laugh, their energy renewed.

One of the men emerges from the apartment holding TOMS GOLD BOX. He hands it to Klancy with a wide grin.

                    MAN (laughing)

          Look what I found, boss. A little treasure.

Klancy opens the box, his smile widening as he examines its contents.

                    KLANCY (quietly, to himself)

          Not bad, Wagner. Not bad.

He turns and walks away, pocketing the box. Nancy and Sandra are dragged down the hallway, their screams and Sandra's sobs echoing as they disappear into the chaos.

FADE OUT.

INT. APARTMENT STAIRWELL – NIGHT

The STAIRWELL is a scene of carnage. DEAD and WOUNDED bodies lie scattered, pools of blood spreading across the floor. The faint moans of survivors mix with the hurried footsteps of MEN roughly herding Nancy and Sandra down the stairs. Nancy clutches Sandra tightly, shielding her as best she can while stumbling forward.

MAN 1   (loud, aggressive)

Move it! Let's go, no time to waste.

Another MAN carries a GAS CAN, splashing its contents liberally into rooms and over the bodies. The sharp stench of gasoline fills the air.

MAN 2 (laughing, mocking)

This is gonna be one hell of a fireball.

EXT. APARTMENT BUILDING – NIGHT

Outside, Paul Klancy lights a CIGARETTE with a calm, almost detached demeanor. The flame of his LIGHTER flickers briefly before he casually tosses it into one of the gasoline-soaked rooms.

KLANCY (calmly, almost

indifferent) TIme to wrap
this up.

The gasoline ignites INSTANTLY, flames roaring to life and spreading rapidly. Smoke begins to pour out of the windows as the fire engulfs the building.

INT. APARTMENT BUILDING – NIGHT

The flames race through the rooms, devouring everything in their path. SCREAMS echo from the upper floors – desperate cries of those trapped inside, with no way out.

191

EXT. APARTMENT BUILDING – NIGHT

The men exit the building, laughing and hollering as the flames rise higher. They roughly shove Nancy and Sandra ahead of them.

MAN 3 (laughing, exhilarated)

Now that's a real show, huh?

Nancy glances back at the building, tears streaming down her face, while Sandra sobs with her eyes tightly shut.

The men push Nancy and Sandra into the waiting VEHICLES, slamming the doors shut behind them.

Paul remains outside, calmly smoking his cigarette as he watches the apartment burn. His eyes scan the other houses on the street, a silent message to the neighborhood. He wants everyone to see what happens when someone crosses him.

KLANCY (quietly, to himself)

Maybe they'll listen now.

After taking one last drag from his cigarette, he flicks it to the ground, crushing it under his heel. With a satisfied smirk, he climbs into his CAR.

The convoy drives off into the night as the APARTMENT BUILDING burns violently. The SCREAMS from inside echo in the distance until they fade away with the departing ve-hicles.

FADE OUT.

EXT. APARTMENT BUILDING – NIGHT

As Tom turns onto the STREET, he freezes. His eyes widen at the sight ahead: FLA-MES engulfing his APARTMENT BUILDING, thick SMOKE rising into the night. PO-LICE and FIREFIGHTERS are on the scene, blue lights flashing rhythmically, illumi-nating the horrified CROWD gathered around.

TOM'S THOUGHTS (V.O.) (desperate, trembling)

Sandra... Nancy...

Tom jumps out of his car, pushing through the crowd, his face a mask of panic. The murmurs of the crowd fade into a muffled hum.

> MAN IN THE CROWD (quietly, shocked)

There was still a family inside...

> WOMAN IN THE CROWD (whispering)

It was brutal. No one could've survived that.

Ignoring the voices, Tom fixates on the burning building. Without hesitation, he runs toward the flames.

> FIREFIGHTER 1 (yelling)

Hey! Stop! You can't go in there!

Tom pulls a CLOTH over his mouth and barrels past the firefighters, disappearing into the building.

INT. BURNING APARTMENT BUILDING – NIGHT

The STAIRWELL is a blazing inferno. FLAMES lick the walls, and THICK SMOKE makes breathing nearly impossible. Tom presses the cloth tightly against his face, climbing the groaning, unstable STAIRS. He stumbles over the BODIES of tenants—some shot, others charred by the fire. His face contorts with anguish.

> TOM'S THOUGHTS (V.O.) (agonized)

Sandra... please no...

FIREFIGHTERS rush down the stairs and try to stop him.

> FIREFIGHTER 2 (panicked)

You can't be here! It's too dangerous!

Tom wrenches free, his voice breaking with desperation.

> TOM (yelling)

My daughter's in there!

He pushes forward, tripping but determined. On the SECOND FLOOR, he reaches the HALLWAY, much of it ablaze. Smoke fills the air, but he charges through, coughing but unrelenting.

INT. TOM'S APARTMENT – NIGHT

Tom stumbles into his apartment, nearly unrecognizable under the smoke and flames. The furniture is scorched, and the heat is suffocating. His eyes dart frantically around.

>   TOM (loud, broken voice)

>   Sandra! Nancy!

Suddenly, his gaze lands on something: SANDRA'S DOLL, half-burned, lying on the floor.

He picks it up with trembling hands, his shoulders slumping. Falling to his knees, he clutches the doll tightly, tears streaming down his face.

>   TOM (CONT'D) (softly, broken)

>   Sandra... no...

His strength fades, and he collapses onto the floor, smoke swirling around him.

INT. BURNING APARTMENT BUILDING – NIGHT

Two FIREFIGHTERS burst into the apartment, spotting Tom on the floor. One shakes his head grimly.

>   FIREFIGHTER 3 (firmly)

>   We need to get him out. Now!

They grab Tom under his arms and drag him out of the apartment.

EXT. APARTMENT BUILDING – NIGHT

The firefighters carry Tom out of the building. His face is covered in soot, his eyes vacant, still clutching the doll. The CROWD falls silent as Tom is laid on a stretcher by

PARAMEDICS.

The camera lingers on the burning BUILDING, flames roaring and screams echoing faintly from inside. The image of the inferno holds as Tom's faint coughing is the last sound before the scene ends.

FADE OUT.

EXT. STREET OUTSIDE THE APARTMENT BUILDING – NIGHT

Tom sits on the edge of an AMBULANCE, an OXYGEN MASK over his face. His soot-covered hands tremble slightly as he clutches Sandra's doll tightly. Paramedics check on him, but his distant gaze shows he's elsewhere, lost in grief and rage.

A NEIGHBOR from the building next door hesitantly approaches, unsure if he should speak. Clearing his throat, he steps closer.

                    NEIGHBOR (quietly, cautiously)

        Wagner... I saw something.

Tom looks up, his eyes locking onto the man with a piercing intensity. The neighbor continues, his voice shaky with fear and regret.

                    NEIGHBOR (CONT'D) (trembling)

        Paul Klancy... he and his men... they took two wo-
        men. One of them... was your daughter, wasn't it?

Tom freezes. His fists clench, and he stands abruptly. His eyes burn with fury and determination.

                    TOM (hoarse, barely

            controlled) Sandra... and
        Nancy.

The neighbor nods hesitantly before retreating. Tom scans the crowd and spots a familiar face – HIS FORMER PARTNER, MASTERS. Masters stands on the edge of the scene, talking to other officers, his expression blank.

Tom strides toward him, each step heavy with anger.

TOM (CONT'D) (loud, demanding)

Masters! We need to talk.

Masters turns, startled to see Tom. For a moment, regret flashes across his face before he composes himself.

MASTERS (calmly, almost evasive)

Tom... this isn't the time.

TOM (angrily, forcefully)

Not the time? My daughter and Nancy were taken, and you're just standing here!

Masters sighs, pulling Tom aside, away from prying eyes.

MASTERS (quietly, matter-of-fact)

Tom, I know what happened. But...

we can't do anything. Paul Klancy's protected. Orders from the top.

TOM (stunned, furious)

Protected? How can you...?

Masters raises a hand, his voice firm.

MASTERS (sharply)

This is bigger than you think, Tom. Klancy has people everywhere. If we go after him, we lose. And we lose big.

Tom grabs Masters by the arm, his eyes drilling into him.

TOM (bitterly, intensely)

Then help me. You know how he operates. You know how he thinks. I need weapons. You owe me this, Masters. You owe Sandra this.

Masters hesitates, his gaze softening as he remembers their past. For a moment, he's not just a cop following orders—he's Tom's partner again.

MASTERS (softly, reflective)

Tom... you know this changes everything,
right? There's no coming back from this.

TOM (firmly, without

hesitation)

I passed the point of no return a long time ago.

Masters nods slowly, the internal struggle fading from his face. He glances around
briefly and speaks quietly.

MASTERS (resolutely)

Three hours. Behind the old police bar. I'll bring
what I can.

Tom nods, gratitude and determination in his eyes.

TOM (calmly, resolutely)

Thank you, Masters. You know this isn't just for
me.

Masters sighs, meeting Tom's gaze.

MASTERS (quietly)

I know, Tom. Be careful.

Tom turns and walks away, still clutching the doll tightly. The camera lingers on Masters as he watches Tom leave, shaking his head before picking up his radio.

FADE OUT.

EXT. DARK ALLEY – NIGHT

The ALLEY is silent, dimly lit by the flicker of a SINGLE STREETLIGHT. Tom
stands in the shadows, arms crossed. His posture is tense, his eyes flicking to the
WATCH on his wrist. His expression is a mixture of anger, despair, and determination.

In the distance, the faint sound of an ENGINE grows louder. Tom looks up, his focus sharpening. A CAR turns into the alley, moving slowly, its engine purring softly. It stops beside him, and the DRIVER'S SIDE WINDOW rolls down. Masters' face appears, his expression grave and unreadable.

Masters steps out of the car, the door closing with a muted thud. Without saying a word, he moves to the back of the vehicle and pops the TRUNK. In the glow of the car's rear lights, a cache of WEAPONS is revealed – handguns, rifles, ammunition, and tactical gear.

Tom steps forward, his movements deliberate. He picks up a HANDGUN, checks the MAGAZINE with practiced efficiency, and tucks it into his WAISTBAND. Another PISTOL finds its place in a freshly strapped ANKLE HOLSTER. He selects a SHOTGUN, loads it, and places it in a large, sturdy BAG along with several other RIFLES.

Masters watches silently, his eyes heavy with exhaustion but flickering with a faint sense of loyalty. As Tom zips the bag and sets it on the ground, he turns to face Masters. For a moment, their eyes meet – an unspoken understanding passing between them.

Tom steps closer and pulls Masters into a brief, firm embrace.

> TOM (quietly, his voice raw)

Thank you, Masters.

Masters nods, saying nothing. Tom picks up the bag, slings it over his shoulder, and turns away. Without looking back, he strides down the dark street, his figure gradually swallowed by the shadows.

Masters remains by the car, leaning against it as he watches Tom disappear into the night.

The camera lingers on Masters' face, etched with worry and a trace of guilt.

> FADE OUT.

EXT. DARK STREETS – NIGHT

The CITY is eerily quiet, save for the occasional sound of DISTANT CARS and the faint WHISTLING of WIND through the empty streets. Tom walks steadily, a heavy BAG of WEAPONS in hand. His eyes are sharp, scanning his surroundings with purpose. Every step is deliberate, every movement tense.

Streetlights cast long shadows, stretching Tom's figure against the cracked pavement. His face is focused, a mix of simmering anger and unrelenting determination.

He stops in front of a dimly lit BAR, its neon sign flickering as if on its last breath. Faint MUSIC, the CLINKING of GLASSES, and muted voices filter out from within.

Tom moves toward the DIRTY WINDOW, leaning slightly to peer inside. His eyes narrow as he studies the PATRONS. A group of MEN sits in the corner, laughing boisterously and raising their glasses. Their rough demeanor and visible tattoos catch Tom's attention.

TOM'S THOUGHTS (V.O.) (quietly, tense)

Are they Klancy's guys?

He lingers for a moment, the limited view through the window frustrating his attempts to get a clearer picture. Shifting slightly, he tries to see more of the scene. Finally, he lowers his gaze, steps back, and moves on.

EXT. MORE STREETS – NIGHT

Tom continues down the dimly lit streets, the bag of weapons swinging slightly in his hand. His face remains resolute, though the tension in his body hints at his inner turmoil. The hunt has just begun, and the night stretches endlessly ahead.

FADE OUT.

EXT. MAIN STREET – NIGHT

The MAIN STREET is alive with faint noises, though the atmosphere feels heavy and ominous. A DRUNKEN MAN, mid-30s, stands outside a BAR, a nearly empty beer bottle in hand.

His shirt is wrinkled, and he sways slightly as he urinates on a parked MOTORCYCLE near the entrance, laughing obnoxiously.

DRUNKEN MAN (slurring)

Stupid bike! Hah!

He hurls the empty beer bottle against the WALL of the bar. The BOTTLE SHATTERS with a loud crash, sending SHARDS flying everywhere. He mutters incoherently, waves dismissively, and staggers down the street.

On the opposite side of the road, Tom watches from the shadows. His eyes lock onto the man with a mix of determination and rage. As the drunk stumbles farther down the street, Tom begins to follow, keeping his distance.

EXT. DARK ALLEY – NIGHT

The drunk veers into a quieter area, away from the busy main street. Tom crosses the road and picks up his pace. When the moment feels right, he sprints across and SHOVES the drunk into a DARK ALLEY. The man stumbles and crashes hard onto the PAVEMENT.

                    DRUNKEN MAN (slurring, angrily)

          What the hell...?

As he struggles to roll onto his back, Tom is already on him. Kneeling over the man, Tom grabs him by the COLLAR and hauls him partway up. Without hesitation, he delivers a solid PUNCH to the man's face. The drunk groans in pain.

                    TOM (coldly, sharply)

          Where's Klancy? His headquarters. How many
          men does he have?

The drunk squirms, trying to free himself, but his drunken state leaves him powerless.

                    DRUNKEN MAN (slurring, mocking)

          You... you don't know... who you're messing with...

Tom tightens his grip and lands another, harder PUNCH. Blood trickles from the man's nose.

                    TOM (menacingly, firmly)

          One more time: Where is Klancy?

The drunk stares up at him, still resisting. Tom strikes him again, the blow heavier. The man groans, then finally starts to talk.

                    DRUNKEN MAN (weakly, trembling)

          Okay, okay! His warehouse... at the docks. He's

got... twenty guys there, at least.

Tom's eyes narrow, his grip unwavering.

> TOM (quietly, dangerously)

> How do I get in?

> DRUNKEN MAN (trembling, panicked)

> The back door... it's usually open. No cameras...

Tom pauses, making sure the man has nothing left to say. Then he delivers one final PUNCH, knocking the drunk unconscious. The man collapses onto the pavement, his chest rising and falling heavily.

Tom stands slowly, adjusts his clothes, and casts one last glance at the man. Without a word, he disappears into the shadows of the street.

> FADE OUT.

EXT. DARK STREETS – NIGHT

Tom walks purposefully down the DARK, DESERTED STREETS of the city. His movements are deliberate, his face set with determination and quiet rage. The WIND whistles through the empty streets, accompanied by the faint crunch of his boots on the pavement.

One hand rests on the weapon tucked into his WAISTBAND, ready for whatever lies ahead. His gaze is fixed straight ahead, his resolve unshakable. Tonight, it all ends.

Suddenly, a CAR pulls up beside him, its engine humming softly. Tom stops, his hand instinctively moving closer to his weapon. The DRIVER'S SIDE WINDOW rolls down, revealing MASTERS. His posture is tense, but his eyes are steadier than they've been in years.

> MASTERS   (calmly, reflectively)

> Tom... get in.

Tom stands still, his expression wary, his eyes locked on Masters.

                    TOM   (dryly, cautious)

            What are you doing here, Masters?

Masters exhales deeply, gripping the steering wheel tightly. His words are slow but resolute.

                    MASTERS (earnestly, almost apologetically)

            I've been thinking. I've watched Klancy terrorize this
            city for too long. I should've stopped him years ago...
            but I didn't.

Tom's posture softens slightly, but he remains silent. Masters continues, his
tone growing firmer.

                    MASTERS (CONT'D) (determined)

            I'm putting what's left of my honor and decency on
            the line. I'm not letting you do the job that should've
            been mine all along.

Tom nods slowly, a flicker of relief crossing his face. There's a brief silence before he
reaches for the car door.

                    TOM (calmly, almost relieved)

            Alright, Masters. Let's finish this.

He climbs into the CAR, closing the door firmly behind him. Masters presses the gas
pedal, and the car begins to roll forward. The two men exchange a brief, determined
glance before driving off, their destination clear.

The camera lingers on the car as it fades into the darkness of the night.

                                                    FADE OUT.

EXT. STREET CORNER – NIGHT

A DARK CAR pulls up at the end of a dimly lit STREET. In the pale moonlight, the silhouette of a run-down WAREHOUSE looms ominously. Several of PAUL KLANCY'S
MEN stand guard near the entrance, weapons slung casually over their shoulders. A
flickering streetlight casts erratic shadows on the cracked pavement.

In the cover of darkness, TOM and MASTERS exit the car. Tom pulls out his BAG OF

WEAPONS and silently unzips it. With practiced hands, he selects two HANDGUNS and a PUMPSHOTGUN. Masters opens his TRUNK and arms himself with a HANDGUN and a RIFLE.

                    TOM (quietly, focused)

        Take the shotgun. Head to the back exit. I'll need it
        later.

Masters nods, takes the shotgun, and checks the ammunition. Without another word, he slips into the shadows, making his way toward the BACK ENTRANCE.

EXT. WAREHOUSE – FRONT ENTRANCE – NIGHT

Tom approaches the FRONT ENTRANCE, feigning drunkenness. He stumbles slightly, mumbling incoherent words, a seemingly empty beer bottle clutched in his hand. The guards at the door notice him immediately, their postures tensing.

                    GUARD 1 (impatiently, sharply)

        Hey, get lost! There's nothing here for you!

Tom ignores them, stumbling closer and muttering nonsensically. The guards exchange irritated glances.

                    GUARD 2 (loud, aggressive)

        Get out of here, drunk! Go find another hole to
        crawl into!

Tom stops, lifts the empty bottle like a toast, and slurs:

                    TOM (laughing, drunkenly)

        You guys... are real nice... you know that?

The guards grow annoyed. One steps forward, roughly shoving Tom backward. Tom stumbles but doesn't fall.

                    GUARD 1 (mocking)

        Look at this idiot. Go home before we give you a
        real reason to run!

203

Tom continues to stagger forward, until the second guard shoves him hard in the shoulder. Tom falls to the ground, the bottle rolling noisily away. The guards laugh, their arrogance unchecked.

In an instant, Tom pulls a HANDGUN from his waistband. The gunfire echoes through the street as he takes down the guards with deadly precision. They collapse to the ground, lifeless.

EXT. WAREHOUSE – FRONT ENTRANCE – NIGHT

Tom rises, brushing the dirt off his clothes, and approaches the door. Just as he reaches it, TWO MORE MEN burst out, weapons drawn.

Tom acts without hesitation, taking them down with two swift shots before they can react. Their bodies hit the ground heavily, the doorway left ajar.

Tom exhales deeply, his expression cold and resolute. He steps through the entrance into the WAREHOUSE.

FADE OUT.

INT. WAREHOUSE BACK ENTRANCE – NIGHT

The BACK ENTRANCE of the warehouse is shrouded in shadows, hidden from view. MASTERS crouches near the heavy STEEL DOOR, his SHOTGUN at the ready. The DISTANT ECHO of GUNFIRE from the front of the building reaches his ears, and he nods to himself - the signal is clear.

MASTERS (quietly, determined)

Alright, Wagner. Let's do this.

Masters grabs the door handle and slowly pushes it open, the hinges creaking softly. Just as the door opens wide enough, a MAN leaps out of the darkness, attacking him. A brutal HAND-TO-HAND STRUGGLE ensues.

The ATTACKER grabs for the shotgun, and the two grapple violently. Masters slams the man into the wall, but the attacker fights back, nearly knocking Masters off balance. With a swift motion, Masters forces the barrel of the shotgun against his opponent and fires. The deafening BLAST echoes down the corridor as the attacker collapses to the ground.

Breathing heavily, Masters scans the area briefly before moving cautiously through

204

the NARROW HALLWAY. The walls are bare, lit by flickering overhead lights. His weapon stays raised, his eyes sharp and focused.

INT. WAREHOUSE – ADJOINING ROOM – NIGHT

Masters reaches another DOOR. He carefully pushes it open, his shotgun ready. The moment the door cracks open, BULLETS rip through the frame, narrowly missing his head. WOOD SPLINTERS fly as he ducks back, quickly throwing himself behind a nearby CRATE.

MASTERS (quietly, to himself)

Great. Just what I needed.

He checks his weapon, his hands moving with practiced precision. The footsteps of the SHOOTER echo through the room, the tension thick in the air.

Masters peeks around the crate, his shotgun aimed, and fires in the direction of the incoming bullets. The shooter ducks, and a chaotic GUNFIGHT erupts. BULLETS ricochet off walls and crates, sending splinters and dust into the air.

Masters breathes heavily, his movements calculated. He shifts to a different piece of cover and uses the opportunity to reload. The shooter's bullets come closer, their sound reverberating through the room.

MASTERS (CONT'D) (loudly, mocking)

You're a terrible shot, buddy!

The shooter responds with another volley of gunfire as Masters dives out of cover, returning fire. The room fills with the echo of gunshots, the confrontation reaching its peak.

FADE OUT.

INT. KLANCY'S OFFICE – NIGHT

Paul Klancy's OFFICE is lavish yet ominous. Heavy drapes shroud the windows, and a thick DESK LAMP casts an uneven glow across the massive MAHOGANY DESK. Klancy stands behind the desk, his hands resting firmly on its surface, his sharp eyes glued to a WALL OF SECURITY MONITORS.

The monitors display Tom and Masters making their way through the building.

One screen shows Tom taking down guards near the front entrance, while another shows Masters navigating hallways, engaging Klancy's men in a tense gunfight. The distant sounds of GUNSHOTS and SHOUTS echo faintly from the monitors.

Klancy's brow furrows briefly before his lips curl into a cold, calculated grin.

                    KLANCY (muttering, mockingly)

          Tom Wagner... you shouldn't have done this. Big
          mistake.

BEHIND HIM, five of his MEN stand armed and alert. They've heard the gunfire and are waiting for orders. Klancy turns to face them, his expression hardening.

                    KLANCY (CONT'D) (commanding)

          Find them. Take them out. Now.

The men nod and move to the WEAPONS RACK along the wall. They grab RIFLES and HANDGUNS, loading them methodically and pocketing spare MAGAZINES. Without hesitation, they head for the door. The heavy door slams shut behind them.

Klancy lingers for a moment, reaching into a hidden drawer in his desk. He pulls out two HANDGUNS, inspecting and loading them with practiced precision. Next, he retrieves a PUMP-ACTION SHOTGUN, loading it deliberately, a sinister smile spreading across his face.

He briefly aims the shotgun at one of the monitors showing Tom and speaks as if addressing him directly.

                    KLANCY (CONT'D) (quietly, smirking)

          Let's see how far you get, Wagner.

He slings the shotgun over his shoulder, takes one last look at the monitors, and strides out of the room, the door slamming shut behind him. The office falls silent, bathed in its eerie, flickering light.

                                        FADE OUT.

INT. WAREHOUSE – NIGHT

Tom moves through the maze-like WAREHOUSE. SMOKE and DUST hang in the air, punctuated by short, violent BURSTS of GUNFIRE. With dual HANDGUNS drawn, he navigates cautiously, his every step calculated.

An ATTACKER emerges from the shadows, firing at him. Tom reacts instantly, his shots deadly and precise. The attacker drops.

As Tom advances, a BULLET suddenly tears through his LEG. He collapses to the floor with a GROAN, dragging himself behind a large TABLE. Blood seeps through his pant leg.

> TOM (through gritted teeth, to himself)
>
> Damn it...

Tom tears a strip of fabric from his shirt and hastily ties it around his leg, grimacing in pain. Despite the agony, his resolve remains unshaken. Reloading his weapons, he peeks over the edge of the table, searching for the SHOOTER.

With a swift motion, Tom rolls out from behind the table, landing in a better position. He fires off a clean shot, taking down the attacker. The room falls silent, save for Tom's labored breathing.

INT. ADJOINING ROOM – NIGHT

Tom limps through a door into the NEXT ROOM. At the same moment, MASTERS bursts in from another door. Instinctively, both men raise their weapons, pointing them at each other.

> TOM & MASTERS (simultaneously, startled)
>
> Don't shoot!

A brief silence follows, tension melting into relief. They lower their weapons and duck behind STACKED CRATES for cover.

Masters notices Tom's injured leg and glances at him with concern.

> MASTERS (quietly, concerned)
>
> How bad is it?

Tom dismisses the concern with a wave of his hand.

                    TOM   (calmly, strained)

          Through and through. It won't stop me.

Masters nods, handing Tom the SHOTGUN. Tom takes it, checks the rounds, and
slings it over his shoulder. Both peek cautiously over the crates, assessing the
enemy's position.

BULLETS slam into the crates, sending WOOD SPLINTERS and DUST flying. The attackers keep them pinned down, relentless in their assault.

                    TOM (CONT'D) (quietly, strategizing)

          I'll go right, you go left. On three.

Masters nods, gripping his weapon tightly. The tension is palpable.

                    TOM (CONT'D) (quietly, counting)

          One... two... three.

Together, they spring into action, firing as they move. BULLETS whiz past them, but
Tom and Masters return fire with precision, advancing closer to their enemies.

INT. WAREHOUSE – COVER POINT – NIGHT

After gaining a few METERS, they find cover behind another set of crates. The room is
thick with SMOKE and DEBRIS, every movement fraught with danger.

Tom looks at Masters, their eyes locking in silent determination. Tom nods, and they
both prepare for the next push. GUNFIRE continues to erupt from both sides as the
battle rages on.

                                        FADE OUT.

INT. WAREHOUSE – NIGHT

The ROOM is filled with DUST and SMOKE, the ECHO of DISTANT GUNFIRE reverberating around them. Tom and Masters crouch behind a row of CRATES as bullets
whiz past, splintering the wood around them. Tom glances at Masters, his face tense
but resolute.

TOM (quietly, firmly)

We need to split up. I'm going after Nancy and
Sandra. Klancy is yours.

Masters nods, their eyes locking in silent agreement.

MASTERS (calmly, resolutely)

Do what you have to. I'll handle him.

Tom nods back, gratitude and determination in his expression. Without another word, he
rises and slips through a nearby door, disappearing into the adjoining room. Masters
watches him go for a moment before gripping his shotgun tightly and moving forward.

INT. WAREHOUSE – HALLWAYS AND ROOMS – NIGHT

Masters advances cautiously, his every movement deliberate. He fires methodically, taking down one ATTACKER after another with precision. His demeanor is calm, but the
tension in his face reveals his sharp focus.

As he passes a STACK OF CRATES, he fails to notice PAUL KLANCY hiding behind them. Klancy suddenly lunges, kicking the SHOTGUN from Masters' hands. A
second powerful kick to the chest sends Masters sprawling to the ground.

MASTERS (gasping, furious)

Klancy...!

Masters scrambles for his SECONDARY WEAPON, but Klancy swiftly kicks it away.
With a menacing GRIN, Klancy looms over him and begins pummeling Masters with
brutal punches. Each blow lands with a sickening thud, accompanied by Klancy's
manic laughter.

KLANCY (loud, mocking)

Did you really think you could stop me, you pathetic
fool?!

Masters fights back, trying to shield himself, but Klancy's relentless assault
overwhelms him. Blood streams down Masters' face, his resistance growing weaker
with each strike. Finally, he lies motionless, his breathing shallow.

Klancy steps back, breathing heavily, his eyes wild with triumph. Suddenly, Masters
makes a desperate move, pulling a KNIFE from his boot. Summoning his remaining

strength, he attempts to strike, but Klancy is faster. He wrests the knife from Masters and slashes his THROAT in one swift motion.

> KLANCY (CONT'D) (coldly, quietly)
>
> That was your last mistake.

Masters' body collapses lifelessly to the ground. Klancy wipes the blade clean on Masters' jacket, then sheaths it at his belt. He surveys the room briefly before turning to his MEN, who have been watching in stunned silence.

> KLANCY (CONT'D) (sharply, commanding)
>
> What are you waiting for? Go finish Wagner! This shouldn't be so hard!

The men spring into action, grabbing their weapons and rushing out of the room. Klancy remains behind, staring down at Masters' body with a smug expression.

> KLANCY (CONT'D) (softly, with a sinister grin)
>
> I know what you want, Wagner.

He grabs his shotgun, slinging it over his shoulder. With deliberate steps, he strides through the door, his cold, calculated demeanor revealing his deadly intent.

FADE OUT.

INT. WAREHOUSE – NIGHT

Tom moves cautiously through the STORAGE ROOMS, his gun raised. FOOTSTEPS and faint MURMURS echo through the dark spaces. Behind every door, Klancy's men seem to be waiting to ambush him.

Tom kicks open a door and is immediately fired upon. He dives for cover, returning precise shots that take out the ATTACKER. Sweat drips from his face as he breathes heavily, his focus unshaken.

INT. ROOM WHERE TOM AND MASTERS SPLIT – NIGHT

Tom enters the room where he last saw Masters. His eyes fall on Masters' lifeless body. Blood pools around him. Tom freezes, his hands trembling as he approaches. The BRUTALITY of the scene screams Klancy's name.

TOM (softly, full of rage)

Klancy...

Tom closes his eyes briefly, taking a deep breath to steady himself. With renewed determination, he moves on. He fights through more rooms, taking down three additional ATTACKERS with precision and unrelenting focus.

INT. LONG HALLWAY – NIGHT

Tom steps into a long, dimly lit HALLWAY. At the far end, he sees NANCY and SANDRA, bound and gagged, sitting on the floor. Sandra is quietly crying, while Nancy looks at him with desperate hope.

Tom exhales with relief and is about to run to them when a SIDE DOOR bursts open. PAUL KLANCY steps out, grabbing Sandra and pulling her to her feet. He presses a gun to her head, his grin widening as he locks eyes with Tom.

KLANCY (mocking)

Wagner, Wagner... what did I tell you? Stay out of
my business! And what did you do? Now you have
nothing, and I have everything.

Tom freezes, raising his hands slightly in a placating gesture.

TOM (pleading)

Klancy, let them go. You want me, not them. Let
them go, and I'll face you.

Klancy laughs coldly, the sound echoing through the hallway.

KLANCY (taunting)

Why should I? You've got nothing left to offer.
Everything you had is already mine.

TOM (earnest, firm)

Man to man. No weapons. Let them go.

Klancy's eyes narrow as he studies Tom's injured leg. Slowly, his grin returns.

211

KLANCY (mocking)

With that busted leg? Fine. I love a fair fight.

He shoves Sandra to the ground, where she curls up beside Nancy. Klancy steps forward, pulling a KNIFE from his belt, his smile growing more sinister.

INT. HALLWAY – THE FIGHT – NIGHT

Tom rips off his SHIRT and wraps it around his left arm as a makeshift shield. The FIGHT begins. Klancy strikes with calculated precision, aiming for Tom's vulnerable spots. Tom blocks with his wrapped arm, retaliating with punches. Each move is raw and brutal, the sound of flesh and bone colliding echoing through the space.

Tom suffers several CUTS but lands solid punches in return. The fight is long and evenly matched until Tom delivers a blow that knocks the KNIFE from Klancy's hand. It skids across the floor, stopping at NANCY'S feet.

Nancy quickly grabs the knife and starts cutting her bonds. Meanwhile, Tom and Klancy continue to trade punches, their fight spilling down the hallway. Klancy lands a hard kick, sending Tom crashing through a door into the NEXT ROOM.

INT. ADJOINING ROOM – NIGHT

Tom lies on the floor, gasping for breath, his body wracked with pain. Klancy strides in slowly, standing over him with a triumphant grin.

KLANCY (mocking)

It's over, Wagner. How could you ever think
you'd win?

Klancy pulls a PISTOL from an ANKLE HOLSTER and points it directly at Tom's face. Tom stares up at the barrel, his eyes filled with despair, realizing he's out of options.

A GUNSHOT rings out. Tom flinches, but it's Klancy who staggers back, clutching his stomach. Blood seeps through his fingers as he collapses to the floor, dropping his weapon. His eyes widen in shock as he looks up at Tom.

Tom turns his head and sees NANCY standing in the doorway, a PISTOL in her trembling hands. Her face is a mix of fear, relief, and disbelief.

NANCY (whispering)

Tom...

Tom rises slowly, limping over to her. He gently takes the gun from her hands and pulls her into a comforting embrace.

TOM (softly)

It's over. Thank you.

INT. LONG HALLWAY – NIGHT

Tom and Nancy return to the hallway. Sandra looks up as they approach, her eyes lighting up with joy and relief.

SANDRA (crying, relieved)

Daddy!

Nancy kneels beside Sandra and cuts her free, pulling her into a tight hug. Tom stands nearby, his expression hardening as he gazes into the distance.

NANCY (concerned)

Tom... where are you going?

TOM (calmly, determined)

There's one last thing I need to do.

Nancy and Sandra watch as Tom walks away, disappearing into the shadows.

FADE OUT.

INT. KLANCY'S OFFICE – NIGHT

Tom enters Klancy's OFFICE. The space is luxurious and pristine, a stark contrast to the grimy warehouse. HEAVY DRAPES adorn the walls, a MASSIVE DARK WOOD DESK dominates the room, and an expensive CRYSTAL LAMP casts a warm glow over the opulent furnishings. It's a surreal sight amidst the chaos of the night.

Tom pauses, scanning the room with narrowed eyes. His face reflects a mix of reluctant admiration and deep disdain.

                    TOM (quietly, to himself)

     Impressive... but I know how much blood paid for this.

He moves around the desk, pulling open drawers one by one, rummaging through their contents. Papers, dirty ledgers, and a few HANDGUNS appear, but nothing catches his interest.

One drawer is locked. Tom pauses, glancing around the room. His eyes land on a small SIDE TABLE. He breaks off the METAL HANDLE and returns to the desk, using it as a makeshift LEVER. With a sharp crack, the drawer pops open.

Tom's eyes widen slightly as he finds several CLEAR JARS filled with GOLD. Coins and jewelry gleam under the soft light of the lamp.

                    TOM (CONT'D) (dryly, quietly)

          Jackpot.

He picks up two jars, turning them over in his hands briefly. A small, wry smile forms on his face.

                    TOM (CONT'D) (mockingly)

          That was my gold.

He slips the jars into his POCKETS. Then, he grabs a third jar, weighing it in his hand before smirking.

                    TOM (CONT'D) (with quiet satisfaction)

          And this is the interest.

He stashes the third jar, pushes the drawer shut carelessly, and straightens up. His gaze sweeps the room before landing on a COAT RACK in the corner. A fine JACKET hangs there, pristine and expensive. Without hesitation, Tom takes it, shrugs it on, and throws it casually over his shoulder.

                    TOM (CONT'D) (softly, almost amused)

          Can't let myself catch cold.

With one last glance around the office, Tom turns and walks out. The heavy door swings shut behind him with a low thud.

FADE OUT.

INT. WAREHOUSE – HALLWAY – NIGHT

Tom steps out of Klancy's office and returns to the HALLWAY. Sandra and Nancy are sitting on the floor, holding each other tightly. Both look exhausted but relieved as they see Tom. Sandra jumps up and runs to him.

SANDRA (crying, relieved)

Daddy!

Tom kneels, pulling her into a tight embrace, holding her close. Nancy rises slowly, her expression a mix of gratitude and weariness.

From outside, the DISTANT SOUND OF POLICE SIRENS echoes faintly through the night. Tom freezes for a moment, listening, his expression hardening.

TOM (urgently)

We need to get out of here. We could never explain this.

Nancy nods silently. She takes Sandra's hand while Tom leads the way. Together, they move as quickly as they can down the hallway, past the wreckage of the fight.

INT. WARCI IOUSE – BACK EXIT – NIGHT

Tom guides Nancy and Sandra toward the BACK EXIT. Their footsteps echo in the empty corridors, the sound of the SIRENS growing closer.

Tom carefully opens the door to the back exit, peering outside to check the surroundings. Satisfied, he nods to the others.

TOM (whispering)

Go, quickly.

Nancy and Sandra slip through the door, Tom following close behind and quietly pulling the door shut.

EXT. WAREHOUSE – BACK EXIT – NIGHT

Outside, the night is eerily quiet except for the distant wail of SIRENS. The three move cautiously, sticking to the shadows, every step deliberate. Tom glances over his shoulder frequently, his hand protectively on Sandra's shoulder.

The camera lingers on the dark silhouette of the warehouse as the three figures disappear into the shadows of the night.

FADE OUT.

EXT. STREET – NIGHT

The streets are eerily quiet, except for the occasional WAIL of distant police sirens. Tom, Nancy, and Sandra walk slowly through the DARK STREETS. Tom's FACE is contorted with pain, his injured LEG making every step excruciating. Nancy supports him on one side, while Sandra clings tightly to his other hand.

Finally, they arrive at Foo's old SHOP. The windows are shattered, shelves overturned – the place has been completely looted. The air smells of dust and charred wood. But for now, it offers the three a temporary refuge.

INT. OLD SHOP – BACK ROOM – NIGHT

In the BACK ROOM, they find a moment of reprieve. Nancy searches the room and finds a FIRST AID KIT. She kneels beside Tom, opening the kit and carefully tending to his wounds. Her expression is one of deep concern, her movements gentle yet efficient.

Tom leans against the wall, his face pale with exhaustion. Sandra sits beside him, curled into his arm. Her little shoulders still shake from her earlier sobs, but fatigue slowly takes over. Finally, she falls asleep at Tom's side.

Nancy wipes her hands clean after finishing the last bandage and looks directly at Tom. Her face reflects exhaustion but also a glimmer of hope.

TOM (calmly, with a hint of relief)

A few days ago, I spoke to the captain of the
African Star. He promised me three spots on
his ship.

Nancy freezes. The word "three" echoes in her mind. Her eyes well up with tears, and
her voice trembles as she asks:

NANCY (softly, uncertainly)

Are you saying... you'd take me with you?

Tom takes her hand—the same hand that was just tending his wounds—and holds
it tightly. His gaze is gentle, his voice steady and resolute.

TOM (gently, firmly)

I wouldn't leave without you. Not for anything.

Nancy's lips tremble, and her eyes shine with joy. Slowly, she leans down toward Tom,
and their lips meet in a long, tender KISS. For a moment, the world around them fades
away.

After the kiss, Nancy nestles against Tom's chest, her smile one of pure contentment.
Her eyes slowly close as exhaustion overtakes her.

Tom looks at Sandra, peacefully asleep, then down at Nancy resting against him.
For the first time in a long while, there's a sense of peace. The three remain silent,
waiting for dawn to break.

                                                    FADE OUT.

EXT. CITY STREETS – MORNING

The MORNING SUN fights its way through the gray clouds, casting a soft, deceptive
glow over the ruined CITY STREETS. The AIR is calm, offering a rare moment of
peace after the chaos of the night.

Tom, Nancy, and Sandra step out of the old SHOP and onto the street. Nancy supports
Tom, whose injured leg makes every step a struggle, while Tom holds Sandra's hand.
Their pace is slow but determined.

The street begins to fill with PEOPLE, all heading out to FIND WORK as they do every
morning. Amid the bustling crowd, the three remain inconspicuous. Yet, there's something different about them—a look of HOPE on their faces.

EXT. PATH TO THE HARBOR – MORNING

The three navigate through the city's busy streets. Despite the destruction and despair surrounding them, they wear small smiles. Tom glances at Nancy, supporting him, and Sandra, walking beside him. For a moment, they look like a proper FAMILY—just as people used to be before the storms.

TOM (inner monologue, hopeful)

It's going to be okay. Everything's going to be okay.

As they reach the end of the street, the HARBOR comes into view. The African Star looms large at the DOCK, a beacon of hope and new beginnings.

The camera lingers on their silhouettes as they walk slowly toward the harbor, before the scene fades out.

FADE OUT.

EXT. HARBOR – DOCK – MORNING

The AFRICAN STAR looms like a massive colossus at the DOCK, its towering smokestacks piercing the sky. A large CROWD gathers at the base of the GANGWAY, desperate to get closer. Several SECURITY GUARDS hold them back with firm resolve.

SECURITY GUARD (shouting, repeatedly)

No one boards without a passage!

Tom, supported by Nancy, leads Sandra by the hand. Together, they push their way through the pressing crowd. Determined, Tom makes his way to one of the security guards.

TOM (whispering, firmly)

I need to speak with the captain. Tom Wagner...
with my wife and daughter.

The security guard eyes Tom briefly, then reaches for his RADIO.

SECURITY GUARD (into the radio)

There's a Tom Wagner here with his wife and child.

Says he has a passage.

There's a moment of silence as the guard waits for a response. Finally, he nods, turning back to Tom and clearing the way to the gangway.

SECURITY GUARD (CONT'D) (dryly)

Alright, you're clear. Go ahead.

Tom nods in gratitude and quickly leads Nancy and Sandra up the GANGWAY.

EXT. AFRICAN STAR – ENTRYWAY – MORNING

At the top of the gangway stands the CAPTAIN of the African Star. He greets Tom
with a firm handshake and then turns to Nancy and Sandra with a warm, polite smile.

CAPTAIN (friendly, but sharp)

Tom Wagner. Welcome aboard. And these
must be your wife and daughter. Glad to have
you.

The captain's eyes drift to Tom's injured LEG, his brow furrowing slightly.

CAPTAIN (CONT'D) (concerned)

No luggage?

TOM (dryly, exhausted)

No chance. Had to leave it all behind.

The captain nods knowingly, then offers a reassuring smile.

CAPTAIN (encouraging)

We'll find something. Don't worry.

His gaze shifts to the HARBOR and the CITY beyond, still scarred from the chaos
of the past night. His expression darkens with unease.

CAPTAIN (CONT'D) (thoughtfully, quietly)

Been hearing some troubling things about what's

been happening in the city. Not good.

Tom discreetly pulls two GOLD JARS from his jacket and hands them to the captain. The captain takes them with a slight nod of understanding, a faint, amused twinkle in his eye.

> CAPTAIN (CONT'D) (quietly, with a hint of humor)
>
> Thanks, Wagner. This will go to good use.

The captain straightens and turns to one of the CREWMEN.

> CAPTAIN (CONT'D) (firmly)
>
> Take them to the guest cabin. And make sure they
> don't linger up here. It wouldn't be smart to have
> him so visible on deck.

The crewman nods, motioning for Tom, Nancy, and Sandra to follow. The captain watches them for a moment, his expression serious, before turning back to his duties.

INT. AFRICAN STAR – HALLWAYS – MORNING

The family follows the crewman through the narrow, metallic HALLWAYS of the ship. Their footsteps echo softly, accompanied by the distant hum of the engines. The African Star remains docked, calm and prepared, but not yet ready to depart.

> FADE OUT.

INT. AFRICAN STAR – GUEST CABIN – MORNING

The small GUEST CABIN is simple and functional. A narrow BUNK is pressed against the wall, next to a tiny PORTHOLE letting in dim morning light. An old CLOSET and a small TABLE complete the sparse furnishings. The floor creaks softly with every step.

Tom sits on the bunk, his injured leg stretched out. Nancy leans over him, checking his bandages with a focused, caring expression. Sandra sits at the table, using a worn pencil to draw on a scrap of paper.

> NANCY (gentle but firm)
>
> You need to rest that leg, Tom. It's not going to heal
> if you keep pushing yourself.

TOM   (grinning slightly,

exhausted)

I didn't think we had much of a choice.

Nancy throws him a half-scolding, half-affectionate look as she tightens the bandages.

NANCY (lightly teasing)

You always have an excuse.

Tom manages a faint smile, but his gaze shifts to Sandra. She hums softly to herself, deeply focused on her drawing. For a moment, the world feels normal again.

SANDRA (excitedly, without looking up)

Look, Daddy! I'm drawing our new home.

Tom and Nancy exchange a glance, their faces showing a mix of hope and worry.

TOM (softly, reassuringly)

It's going to be a beautiful place, Sandra. I promise.

KNOCKING ON THE DOOR

The moment is interrupted by a firm KNOCK. Nancy opens the door to reveal a CREWMAN standing outside.

CREWMAN (polite but urgent)

The captain would like to see you. Both of you.

Nancy glances at Tom questioningly. Tom nods and tries to stand, but Nancy stops him.

NANCY (determined)

I'm coming with you. You shouldn't push yourself.

Tom hesitates for a moment before slowly rising, leaning on Nancy for support. Together, they leave the cabin.

INT. AFRICAN STAR – CAPTAIN'S CABIN – MORNING

The CAPTAIN'S CABIN is simple but tidy, with nautical charts spread across a large wooden table in the center of the room. The CAPTAIN stands by the porthole, gazing out at the harbor. He turns as Tom and Nancy enter.

> CAPTAIN (friendly but serious)

Wagner. Glad to see you made it.

His eyes linger briefly on Tom's injured leg.

> CAPTAIN (CONT'D) (concerned)

How's the leg holding up?

> TOM (calmly)

It'll do. What's going on?

The captain gestures toward a WEATHER MAP on the table, showing a massive STORM FRONT heading toward the coast.

> CAPTAIN (matter-of-factly)

We've just received a new forecast. There's an unexpected storm coming in – bigger than the last ones. We have to leave the harbor sooner than planned. A few hours from now.

Nancy's face tightens with concern, while Tom looks tense.

> NANCY (worried)

Is it that bad?

> CAPTAIN (serious)

Yes. If we stay, we risk being trapped here in the storm. And if that happens, no ship is getting out for a long time.

He pauses briefly, meeting Tom's eyes with a steady gaze.

CAPTAIN (CONT'D) (encouragingly)

Don't worry. We have everything we need to make it safely. But I need your cooperation – keep your family calm and be ready when it's time to move.

Tom nods, locking eyes with the captain.

TOM (firmly)

Thank you for taking us on.

The captain nods in return, turning back to the porthole. His gaze drifts over the quiet harbor, bathed in the soft morning light.

CAPTAIN (quietly, almost to himself)

No time to waste.

Tom and Nancy leave the cabin. The camera lingers on the captain, staring out at the approaching storm clouds, before the scene transitions.

FADE OUT.

EXT. HARBOR – EVENING

The sun has set, and the sky is painted in dark shades of gray. The AFRICAN STAR still sits at the DOCK, but the atmosphere is tense. A small, desperate CROWD has gathered near the GANGWAY. Some shout for passage, others silently plead. SECURITY GUARDS stand firm, holding the line against last-ditch attempts to board.

SECURITY GUARDS (sternly)

Stand back! The ship is full!

The noise grows louder. A few people try to break through, but the guards push them back with firm hands and shoulders. In the background, the sound of heavy boots echoes as the GANGWAY is slowly pulled up onto the ship.

EXT. HARBOR – SHIP – EVENING

The GANGWAY disappears onto the deck. Below, the cries and shouts persist, but the ship remains resolute. DOCK WORKERS release the heavy LINES at the BOW and STERN. A loud HISS signals the release.

SHIP'S HORN

The African Star's HORN blares twice, its deep,
resonant tone startling the crowd below. Some
look up in hopelessness, while others bow their
heads in resignation.

Slowly, the ship begins to pull away from the dock. The BOW turns deliberately toward
the OPEN SEA, while the STERN still faces the city.

EXT. SHIP – STERN – EVENING

At the stern, three figures stand close together: TOM, NANCY, and SANDRA. Their silhouettes are outlined against the darkening sky. The city behind them is a shadowy
mass of ruins, and beyond it, a massive STORM FRONT looms on the horizon. Light-
ning flickers in the distance.

TOM (quietly, thoughtfully)

We made it...

Nancy leans into him, her eyes filled with gratitude but also heavy with concern. Sandra
clings to Tom´s arm, silently gazing back at the city.

NANCY (softly)

But they didn´t...

The three of them stare back at the city, at the people left behind, and at the approaching storm. Their relief at escaping is tinged with sorrow and unease.

The ship glides further into the SEA, as the storm on the horizon grows ever closer.
The three remain at the stern, watching as the city fades into darkness.

FADE OUT.   END   CREDITS